教材项目规划小组

严美华　　姜明宝　　王立峰
田小刚　　崔邦焱　　俞晓敏
赵国成　　宋永波　　郭　鹏

教材编写委员会

主　任：陶黎铭
副主任：陈光磊　　吴叔平
成　员：陈光磊　　高顺全　　陶黎铭
　　　　吴金利　　吴叔平　　吴中伟

顾　问　Richard King
　　　　Helen Xiaoyan Wu
　　　　Robert S. Chen

中国国家对外汉语教学领导小组办公室规划教材

Project of NOTCFL of the People's Republic of China

Dāngdài Zhōngwén

当 代 中 文

Contemporary Chinese

Hànzì Běn
汉字本

1

CHARACTER BOOK
Volume One

主　　编：吴中伟

编　　者：吴中伟　吴叔平
　　　　　高顺全　吴金利

翻　　译：徐　蔚
　　　　　Yvonne L. Walls　Jan W. Walls

译文审订：Jerry Schmidt

华语教学出版社
SINOLINGUA

First Edition   2003
Seventh Printing   2011

ISBN 978-7-80052-881-1
Copyright 2003 by Sinolingua
Published by Sinolingua
24 Baiwanzhuang Road, Beijing 100037, China
Tel: (86) 10-68320585 68997826
Fax: (86) 10-68997826 68326333
http:// www.sinolingua.com.cn
E-mail: hyjx@sinolingua.com.cn
Printed by Beijing Foreign Languages Printing House

Printed in the People's Republic of China

Mùlù
目 录
Contents

Fundamental strokes

Héng   The horizontal stroke
        (from left to right)

一

Shù   The vertical stroke
        (from top to bottom)

丨

Piě   The left descending stroke

丿

Diǎn   The dot

丶

Nà   The right descending stroke

乀

Tí   The upcutting stroke

／

Zhé   The bending strokes

乛 乚

Gōu   The hooked strokes

乛 亅 丨 乀

Rules of stroke order

First left, then right

丿 八

First top, then bottom

一 二 三

First horizontal, then vertical

一 十

The outside, then the inside

丿 刀 月 月

Close after filling the frame

丨 冂 冂 冃 用 国 国 国

first center, then sides

亅 小 小

First the main body, then join it together

丶 冂 口 中

Names of some common radicals

亻	dānrénpáng	人	person, man	休	钅	jīnzìpáng	金	metal, gold	钱
彳	shuāngrénpáng		to pace	行	礻	shìzìpáng	示	god	视
女	nǚzìpáng	女	woman	妈	衤	yīzìpáng	衣	clothes	裤
氵	sāndiǎnshuǐ	水	water	河	足	zúzìpáng	足	foot	路
木	mùzìpáng	木	tree, wood	林	马	mǎzìpáng	马（馬）	horse	骑
讠	yánzìpáng	言	words, speech	语	疒	bìngzìpáng	病	sickness	疼
口	kǒuzìpáng		mouth	吃	刂	lìdāo	刀	knife	到
饣	shízìpáng	食	eat, food	饭	攵	fǎnwén	文	culture	教
日	rìzìpáng		sun	明	艹	cǎozìtóu		grass	茶
目	mùzìpáng		eye	眼	𥫗	zhúzìtóu	竹	bamboo	等
忄	shùxīnpáng	心	heart	忙	宀	bǎogàir		roof	家
土	títǔpáng	土	earth, soil	地	穴	xuébǎogàir	穴	cave	空
扌	tíshǒupáng	手	hand	打	冖	tūbǎogàir		to cover	写
阝	zuǒ'ěrpáng	阜	hill	附	𭕄	xuézìtóu			学
阝	yòu'ěrpáng	邑	city	都	𭕄	chángzìtóu			常
子	zǐzìpáng	子	son, child	孩	灬	sìdiǎndǐ	火	fire	点
纟	jiǎosīpáng	丝	silk	红	心	xīnzìdǐ	心	heart	您
王	wángzìpáng	玉	jade	玩	辶	zǒuzhī	走	walk	这
车	chēzìpáng	车（車）	cart	较	囗	kǒuzìkuāng	囗	enclosure	国
火	huǒzìpáng	火	fire	灯					

0. Preparation

0.1

汉字 Hànzì **Chinese characters**

yī	èr	sān	sì	wǔ
一	二	三	四	五
one	two	three	four	five

liù	qī	bā	jiǔ	shí
六	七	八	九	十
six	seven	eight	nine	ten

一　　　二　　　三　　　四　　　五

六　　　七　　　八　　　九　　　十

笔画 Bǐhuà **Strokes**

All *Hanzi* are composed of strokes. Here are the basic ones.

stroke	direction	name	example
一	→	Héng	二
丨	↓	Shù	十
丿	↙	Piě	八
丶	↘	Diǎn	六
㇏	↘	Nà	八

There are nearly 30 kinds of strokes altogether. The other strokes are based on the basic strokes above. Here are some of them:

stroke	direction	name	example
㇆	↱	Héngzhé	口
㇄	↳	Shùwān	四
㇂	↳	Shùwāngōu	七
㇈	⟿	Héngzhéwāngōu	九

In each of the following lines, the first character is in the Sòngtǐ form, which is the commonest printed form. The second one is in the Zhèngkǎi form, which is a form used when writing with a Chinese brush (Máobǐ). The third one is the form used when writing with a pen (shǒuxiětǐ)

Sòngtǐ	Zhèngkǎi	Shǒuxiětǐ	Pīnyīn	stroke order			
一	一	一	yī	一			
二	二	二	èr	二	二		
三	三	三	sān	三	三	三	
四	四	四	sì	四	四	四	四
				四			
五	五	五	wǔ	五	五	五	五
六	六	六	liù	六	六	六	六
七	七	七	qī	七	七		
八	八	八	bā	八	八		
九	九	九	jiǔ	九	九		
十	十	十	shí	十	十		

With a history of some four thousand years, Chinese characters are one of the earliest forms of writing in the world. Chinese characters have made great contributions to the development of Chinese civilization and are still important today.

About 60,000 Chinese characters have been used at one time or another. However, if we eliminate alternate forms and "dead" characters no longer in use, the number being used today total between ten and twenty thousand. But even this figure is not truly representative of the number of characters that must be learned. In fact, 6000 characters are quite sufficient for general reading. The characters taught here are the ones most frequently used in daily life. If you know 2400 of the most frequently used characters, you will be able to recognize 99% of the characters you meet in most newspapers and magazines. And if you know 3800 characters, you will be able to recognize 99.9% of such characters.

0.2

汉字 Hànzì **Chinese characters**

rén	dà	kǒu	zhōng	xiǎo	shàng	xià
人	大	口	中	小	上	下
people	big	mouth	middle	small	above	below

笔画 Bǐhuà **Strokes**

stroke	direction	name	example
亅	↓	Shùgōu	小

笔顺 Bǐshùn **Stroke order**

Chinese character should be written in the correct stroke order. This will ensure correctness, increase the speed of writing and be helpful when looking up characters in a dictionary. The main rules of stroke order are:

First left, then right   e.g.   八   八   八

First top, then bottom   e.g.   三   三   三   三

first horizontal, then vertical	e.g.	十	十	十		
"Let him come in, then close the door"	e.g.	四	四	四	四	四
		四				
First center, then sides	e.g.	小	小	小	小	
First the main body, then join it together	e.g.	中	中	中	中	中

………….

The rules may appear excessively complex, but stroke order can be summed up by the first two rules: first left, then right; first top, then bottom.

写字　xiězì　**Writing**

Sòngtǐ	Zhèngkǎi	Shǒuxiětǐ	Pīnyīn	stroke order		
人	人	人	rén	人	人	
大	大	大	dà	大	大	大
口	口	口	kǒu	口	口	口
中	中	中	zhōng	中	中	中	中
小	小	小	xiǎo	小	小	小
上	上	上	shàng	上	上	上
下	下	下	xià	下	下	下

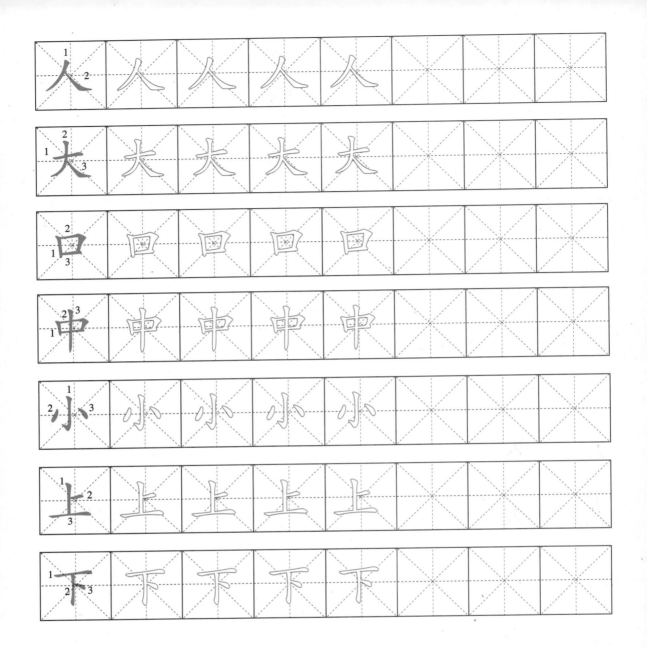

0.3

汉字　Hànzì　Chinese characters

guó	xué	xí	Hàn
国	学	习习习	汉
country	learn	learn	Han

中国	学习	汉语
Zhōngguó	xuéxí	Hànyǔ
China	learn, study	Chinese language

yǔ	wén	xiě	zì
语	文	写 写写写	字 字
language	language	write	character

汉语	中文		汉字
Hànyǔ	Zhōngwén		Hànzì
Chinese language	Chinese language		Chinese character

笔画 Bǐhuà **Strokes**

stroke	direction	name	example
 フ フ ヽ ζ 〜 ノ	↘ ↙ ↗ ↙ → ↓	héngzhégōu héngpiě tí héngzhétí hénggōu wāngōu	习 又 汉、习 语 学 学

部件 Bùjiàn **Component**

Except for the single ones, the majority of Chinese characters can be decomposed into smaller components.

e.g.

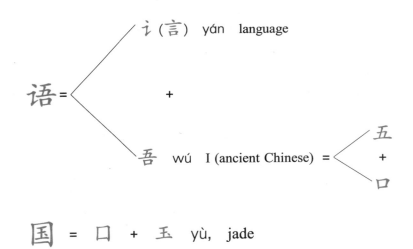

语 = 讠（言） yán language
   + 吾 wú I (ancient Chinese) = 五 + 口

国 = 口 + 玉 yù, jade

结构 Jiégòu **Structure**

A character is more or less square in form, which is why it is called a fāngkuàizì. ("square" or "block-style" character). When we put a character in a box, we must position the components properly so that it looks balanced and clear.   Characters can be classified into four categories on the basis of their structure.

structure	shape	percent	example
Single structure		3%	口
Right-left structure	▯	65%	汉
Over-under structure	▯	23%	学
Enclosing structure	▯	9%	国

写字   xiězì   **Writing**

Sòngtǐ	Zhèngkǎi	Shǒuxiětǐ	Pīnyīn	stroke order
国	国	国	guó	国 国 国 国 国 国 国 国
学	学	学	xué	学 学 学 学 学 学 学 学
习	习	习	xí	习 习 习
汉	汉	汉	hàn	汉 汉 汉 汉 汉

语	语	**语**	yǔ	语	语	语	语
				语	语	语	语
文	文	**文**	wén	文	文	文	文
写	写	**写**	xiě	写	写	写	写	写
字	字	**字**	zì	字	字	字	字	字
				字			

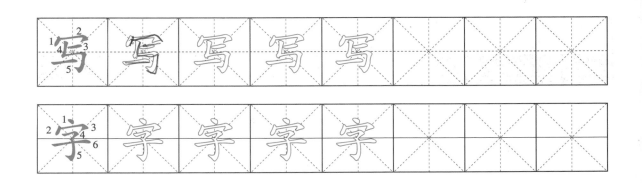

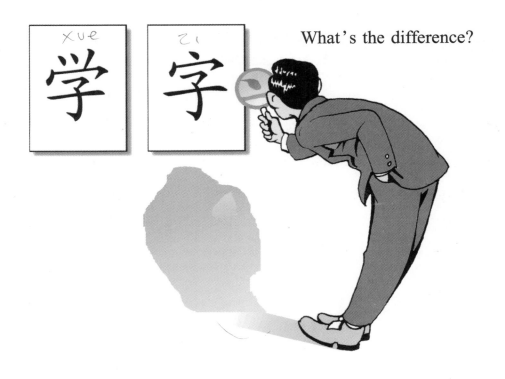

What's the difference?

0.4

汉字　Hànzì　**Chinese characters**

nǚ	zǐ	hǎo	shuǐ	mén	wáng
女	子	好	水	门	王
female	son,child	good	water	door	king
	女子			门口	国王
	nǚzǐ			ménkǒu	guówáng
	woman			doorway	king

笔画　Bǐhuà　**Strokes**

stroke	direction	name	example
㇐	↙	piědiǎn	女

写字　xiězì　**Writing**

Sòngtǐ	Zhèngkǎi	Shǒuxiětǐ	Pīnyīn	stroke order	
女	女	女	nǚ	女　女　女	

子	子	子	zǐ	子	子	子	
好	好	好	hǎo	好	好	好	好
				好	好		
水	水	水	shuǐ	水	水	水	水
门	门	门	mén	门	门	门	
王	王	王	Wáng	王	王	王	王

女 女 女 女 女 女 女 女

子 子 子 子 子 子 子 子

好 好 好 好 好 好 好 好

水 水 水 水 水 水 水 水

门 门 门 门 门 门 门 门

王 王 王 王 王 王 王 王

Two characters put together can frequently make a new character, e.g. 好.
Two characters put together can also make a word, e.g.

女子　nǚzǐ　woman

子女　zǐnǚ　son and daughter

好(hǎo, good) is only one character, so it can only occupy one box when writing in an exercise

book. The components 女 and 子 in 好 can only occupy half the size of a box. Since 女子 (nǚzǐ,

woman) form a word of two characters, 女 and 子 should each be written in a box in an exercise

book.

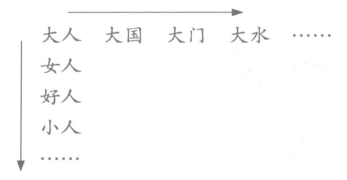

字和词　Zì(characters) and　Cí(words)

A Zì can be a Cí by itself, e.g. 人.
A Zì can also be a component of a Cí, e.g. 人口 (population, two zì but one cí).
Some frequently used characters can produce many words. E.g. 大, 人

大人　大国　大门　大水　……
女人
好人
小人
……

We can often guess the meaning of a compound word by examining its characters, e.g. 女人 *a
female person*, woman. But it is not always possible to do so because sometimes a word cannot be
taken literally, e.g. 小人, *small / little person*, actually means *a mean person*, *villain*.

However, some Zì can never be a Cí in modern Chinese. They can only form Cí in combination
with another Zì, e.g. the 习 in 学习, and 语 in 汉语. They are called bound morphemes and will be
marked Ⓑ in this book.

The Evolution of *Hanzi*

Over the centuries, not only the forms of characters but also their meanings, pronunciations and uses have changed to a greater or lesser extent. For example, the character 子 was not pronounced "zǐ" in ancient times and it could be used alone to refer to both sons and daughters, but now 子 (pronounced zǐ in Mandarin) is only used to make words together with other characters , e.g. 儿子，子女，in which it only indicates sons. Furthermore, 好 originally meant "beautiful" instead of "good" as it does today.

A character may have had different pronunciations in different periods of history, and it may have very different readings in different dialects now. It is more difficult to know the ancient pronunciations than the ancient meanings of characters. We may not know how a character was pronounced, but we still can "read" the ancient literature in characters, if we have some knowledge about the ancient language. People from areas of different dialects may not be able to communicate with each other if they don't speak Mandarin(Pǔtōnghuà), but they still can understand each other by writing in characters.

0.5

汉字　Hànzì　**Chinese characters**

rì	yuè	mù	mǎ	tián
日 日	月 月	木 木	马 马	田 田
sun	moon	wood	horse	field

tiān	míng	lín	mā	hé
天 天	明 明	林 林	妈 妈	河 河
sky	bright	woods	mother	river

笔画　Bǐhuà　**Strokes**

stroke	direction	name	example
𠃋	⚡	shùzhézhégōu	马

写字　xiězì　**Writing**

Sòngtǐ	Zhèngkǎi	Shǒuxiětǐ	Pīnyīn	stroke order			
日	日	日	rì	日	日	日	日

月	月	月	yuè	月	月	月	月
木	木	木	mù	木	木	木	木
马	马	马	mǎ	马	马	马	
田	田	田	tián	田	田	田	田
天	天	天	tiān	天	天	天	天
明	明	明	míng	明	明	明	明
				明	明	明	明
林	林	林	lín	林	林	林	林
				林	林	林	林
妈	妈	妈	mā	妈	妈	妈	妈
				妈	妈		
河	河	河	hé	河	河	河	河
				河	河	河	河

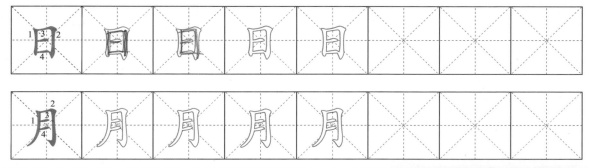

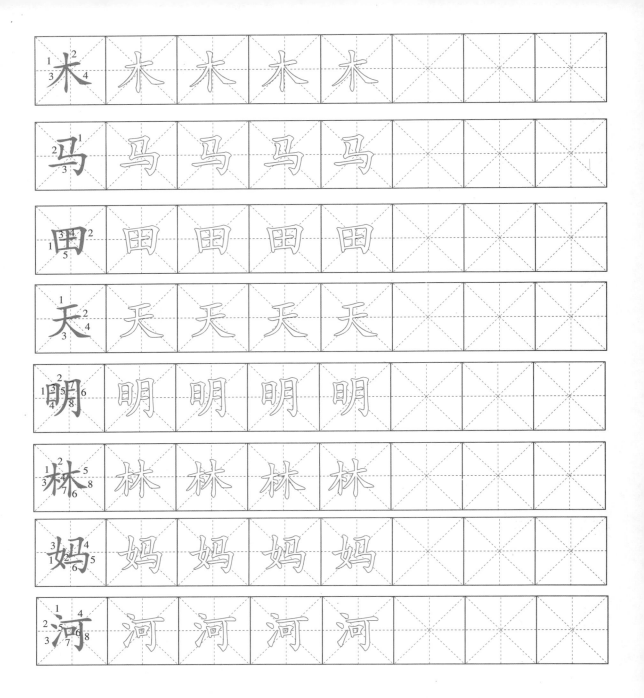

Structure of Ancient Characters

Understanding the structure of ancient Chinese characters can help us understand their origin and meaning. Most Chinese characters were formed in one of four different ways.

Xiàngxíng, pictographic. A pictographic character represents the object it refers to in stylized form. About 5% of characters belong to this category.

日　rì　sun, day

It is a pictograph of the "sun". By extension, it means "daytime" or "day".

月　yuè　moon, month

It is a pictograph of the "moon".

木　mù　tree, wood

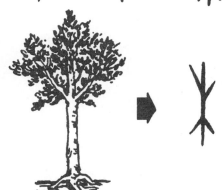

This is a pictograph of a tree with branches above and roots below.

水　shuǐ water

This is a pictograph in which the winding center represents flowing water and the dots on the sides signify drops of water or waves.

田　tián　field

It represents four fields.

马　mǎ horse

It is a vivid depiction of a horse.

人　rén　person

This pitograph shows a man standing with one hand extended forward.

口　kǒu　mouth

It shows a person's mouth.

门　mén　door

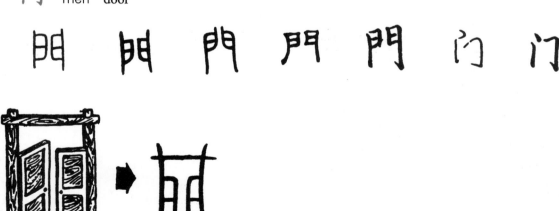

It resembles two shutters.

子　zǐ　child

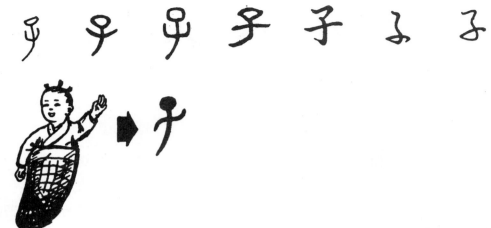

It shows a baby with a head and hands and two legs wrapped in swaddling clothes.

女　nǚ　female

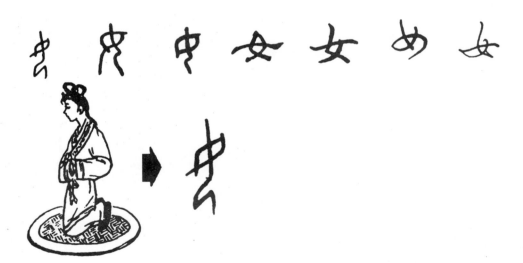

This pictograph shows a woman kneeling on a straw mat, hands folded gently on her stomach.

Zhǐshì, Indicative. Indicative characters use symbols to indicate abstract meanings. There are not many characters in this category.

上　shàng　above

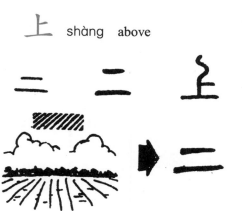

It was originally composed of two horizontal lines, the lower indicating the horizon, the upper the indicative symbol. Its form gradually changed so that it would be distinguished from 二 two.

中　zhōng　middle

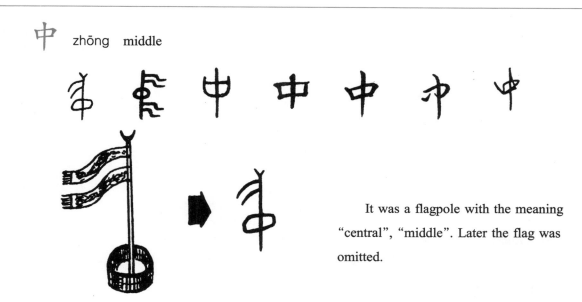

It was a flagpole with the meaning "central", "middle". Later the flag was omitted.

下　xià　below

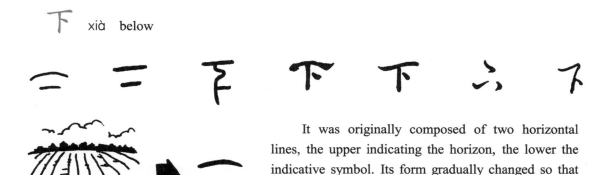

It was originally composed of two horizontal lines, the upper indicating the horizon, the lower the indicative symbol. Its form gradually changed so that it would be distinguished from 二 two.

天 tiān sky, day

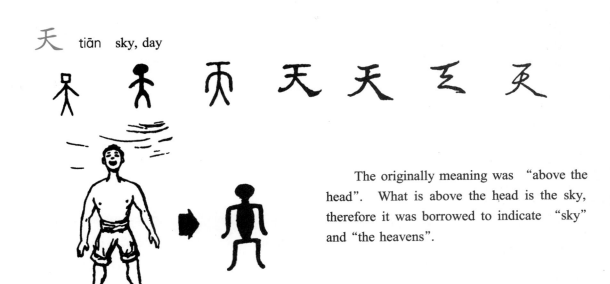

The originally meaning was "above the head". What is above the head is the sky, therefore it was borrowed to indicate "sky" and "the heavens".

Huìyì, Associative. Associative characters result from the combination of two or more elements to create a new character with a new meaning.

明　míng　bright　日 + 月
林　lín　woods　木 + 木
休　xiū　rest　人 + 木
男　nán　male　田 + 力

Xíngshēng, Picto-phonetic. A picto-phonetic character is composed of a part indicating its meaning and the other part indicating its pronunciation. Characters of this kind account for more than 80% of all Chinese characters.

妈　mā　mother　女 (picto element) + 马 (phonetic element)
河　hé　river　水 (picto element) + 可 (phonetic element)
们　mén　a suffix for plural pronouns/ nouns

人 (picto element) + 门 (phonetic element)

问　wèn　ask　门 (phonetic element) + 口 (picto element)

As we can see from the above examples, owing to the changes that have occurred over long periods of development in language and writing, phonetic elements and picto elements have to a great extent lost their ability to represent pronunciation and meaning exactly.

0.6

Review 汉字(41)

一 二 三 四 五 六 七 八 九 十

土 不 大 中 小 人 口

国 学 习 汉 语 文 写 字

女 子 好 水 门 王

白 月 木 马 田 天 明 林 妈 河

偏旁 Piānpáng **Radicals**

The radical of a Chinese character is usually related to its meaning. If we know the names and meanings of radicals we can memorize Chinese characters more easily. The following are several common radicals:

亻 dānrénpáng (person): 们 休

女 nǚzìpáng (woman): 妈 好

氵 sāndiǎnshuǐ (water): 汉 河

讠 yánzìpáng (speech): 语

木 mùzìpáng (tree, wood): 林

日 rìzìpáng (sun): 明

一、写出含有下列偏旁的汉字：

Write Chinese characters containing the following radicals:

女　(nǚzìpáng)

氵　(sāndiǎnshuǐ)

讠　(yánzìpáng)

木　(mùzìpáng)

日　(rìzìpáng)

二、在下面的汉字基础上增加笔画,把它变成另外一个汉字：

Add strokes to the following Chinese characters so that they change into other Chinese characters:

e.g.　一 ➡ 十

人　大　口　十

三、补上丢失的笔画,使之成为一个汉字：

Supply the missing strokes to the following to produce Chinese characters:

⊥　丁　门　水　马　学　习　乙

四、学习书写自己国家的名字和自己的中文名字：

Learn to write your name and your country's name in Chinese：

五、猜一猜下面的汉字组合是什么意思：

Guess the meanings of the following combinations of Chinese characters:

好子女　子女好

女子好　好女子

水中月　天上人

女人国小国王天天学习汉语口语。

繁体字和简体字　Fántǐzì **and** Jiǎntǐzì

Traditional characters and simplified chararters

A considerable number of Chinese characters have numerous strokes and complex structures, which causes difficulties in learning, remembering and writing them. As a result, variants with fewer strokes and simpler structures have come into being over the centuries. These are known as jiǎntǐzì (simplified characters / simple form of the characters) as opposed to the original fántǐzì (traditional characters / complex form of the characters).

Chinese characters have a long history of simplification, which in fact started almost from their beginning. Simplified characters have even been found in the oracle bone inscriptions of the *Shang* Dynasty more than three thousand years ago. After the founding of the People's Republic of China in 1949, simplified characters already in wide currency began to be collected and standardized. In 1956 the government published Hànzì Jiǎnhuà Fāng'àn (A Scheme for Simplifying Chinese Characters), and in 1964 a further list, Jiǎnhuàzì Zǒngbiǎo (Complete List of Simplified Characters), containing a total of 2236 simplified characters, was published.

Some examples of 繁体字(fántǐzì) and 简体字(jiǎntǐzì):

馬	媽	門	學
马	妈	门	学

習	漢	語	國
习	汉	语	国
xi	han	yu	guo

實諦傳授之賓和其妙理

之苑斯闡結集之侶揚其

之岸先登鳥筆記言總持

之簡暨乎鶴林稅斬涅槃

然則紹宣神典幽替玄宗

跨生摹以遐騫追安什而

曾驚可以聲融繡石采絢

雕圖則於我法師而見之

Master Daoyin's Tablet
by Ouyang Tong of the Tang Dynasty

Dì-yī Kè

第一课

Lesson One

汉字

(Ⓑ = bound morpheme, the figure after the character stands for the stroke number of the character.)

1. 您   11 nín   a polite form for 你 (nǐ)

您 您 您 您 您 您 您 您 您 您 您

你 + 心

您好!

您 您 您 您 您

Note: 心(xīn), heart is added to 你 to indicate respect.

2. * 贵 9 guì honourable   贵

贵 贵 贵 贵 贵 贵 贵 贵 贵

中 + 一 + 贝

贵 贵 贵 贵

您贵姓?

Note: 贵 originally meant "valuable". 贝 (*bèi*) means "shell". In ancient times shells were used as money.

---

3. 姓　8　xìng　surname, be surnamed

姓 姓 姓 姓 姓 姓 姓 姓

女 ＋ 生

我姓王。您贵姓？你姓什么？

---

4. 我　7　wǒ　I, me

我 我 我 我 我 我 我

Note: the fouth stroke is *tí* (from down to up), not *piě*. Do not forget the last *diǎn* of the character.

---

5. 呢　8　ne

呢 呢 呢 呢 呢 呢 呢 呢

口 ＋ 尼

我是中国人，你呢？

---

6. 是　9　shì　be

是 是 是 是 是 是 是 是 是

日 ＋ 疋

他是我同学。

7. 吗　6　ma　a question marker for a yes-or-no question　嗎

　　吗　吗　吗　吗　吗　吗

　　口　+　马　吗　吗　吗　吗　吗　吗
　　　　　　　　　　吗

　　你是中国人吗?

8. 不　4　bù　no, not

　　不　不　不　不　　不　不　不　不
　　　　　　　　　　　　不　不　不　不

　　我不是法国人。我不学习法语。

　　　　　*　　　　　*　　　　　*　　　　　*

9. 同　6　Ⓑ　tóng　together, same

　　同　同　同　同　同　同　同　同　同　同　同　同　同
　　　　　　　　　　　　　同　同　同　同　同　同

　　同学

10. 们　5　Ⓑ　men　們　们　们　们

　　们　们　们　们　们　们　们　们

　　亻　+　门

　　你们　我们　他们　同学们

11. 老　6　lǎo　old

　　老　老　老　老　老　老

　　耂　+　匕　　老　老

　　老人　老师　　老　老
　　我们的老师不老。

It shows an old man leaning on a stick.

12. 师 6 Ⓑ shī teacher, master 師

   师 师 师 师 师 师

   丿 + 帀

   ◆ 老师

---

13. 叫 5 jiào call

   叫 叫 叫 叫 叫

   口 + 丩

   ◆ 你叫什么名字？　我们叫她王老师。
      什么叫"国王"，什么叫"王国"？

---

14. 你 7 nǐ you

   你 你 你 你 你 你 你

   亻 + 尔

---

15. 什 4 Ⓑ shén

   什 什 什 什

   亻 + 十

   ◆ 什么

---

16. 么 3 Ⓑ me 麽

   么 么 么

   ◆ 什么

17. 名 6 Ⓑ míng name

名 夕 夕 名 名 名

夕 + 口

姓名　名字

It is composed of 夕 (xī), night and 口 (kǒu), mouth. At night a person in the distance can only be distinguished if he answers to the calling of his name.

18. * 哪 9 nǎ which

丨 哪 哪 哪 哪 哪 哪 哪 哪

口 + 那

你是哪国人？

19. 也 3 yě also, too

也 也 也

他也不是中国人。他也学习汉语。

20. 说 9 shuō say 说

说 说 说 说 说 说 说 说 说

讠 + 兑

你说什么？　我们都说汉语。

说一不二 means what one says　stand by one's word.

21. * 英 8 Ⓑ Yīng

英 英 英 英 英 英 英 英

艹 + 央

Note: In ancient Chinese 英 meant "flower". Here it is the transliteration of "England" and

"English".

◆ 英国　英语　英文

---

22. 还 7 hái 還

ⅷ 还 还 还 还 还 还 还

✕ 不 ＋ 辶

◆ 还是

---

23. * 法 8 Ⓑ fǎ

ⅷ 法 法 法 法 法 法 法 法

◁ 氵 ＋ 去

Note: 法 means "law" or "method". Here it is the transliteration of "France" and "French".

◆ 法国　法语　法文

---

24. 都 10 dōu all, both

ⅷ 都 都 都 都 都 都 都 都 都 都

◁ 者 ＋ 阝

◆ 我们都不是中国人。　我们都学习汉语。

---

25. 只 5 zhǐ only

ⅷ 只 只 只 只 只

◆ 她只说英语,我只说汉语。

26. 他　5　tā　he, him

◁▷ 他　他　他　他　他

◁▷ 亻　＋　也

27. 她　6　tā　she, her

◁▷ 她　她　她　如　她　她

◁▷ 女　＋　也

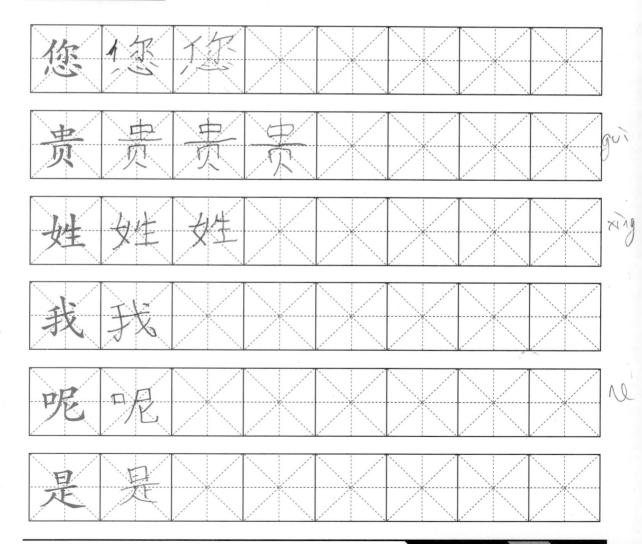

您 您 您

贵 贵 贵 贵　　　　　　　gùi

姓 姓 姓　　　　　　　　xìng

我 我

呢 呢　　　　　　　　　ne

是 是

吗	吗	吗	吗	吗			

bù
不	不	不					

Tóng
(together/same)
同	同	同	同				

们							

lao
老	老						

Shi
师	师						

Jiao
叫	叫	叫	叫	叫	叫		

你							

什							

么							

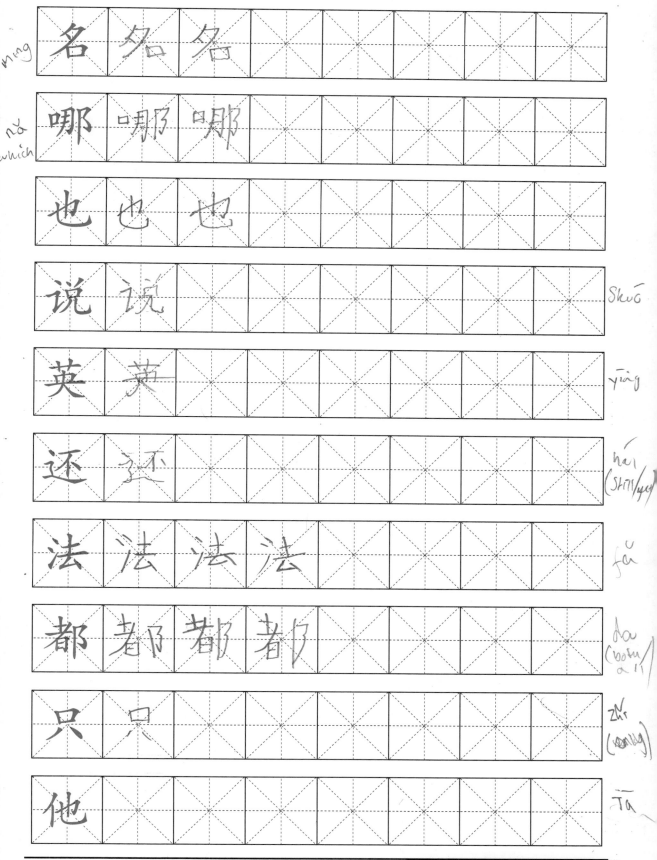

名	名	名						
哪	哪	哪						
也	也	也						
说	说							
英	英							
还	还							
法	法	法	法					
都	都	都	都					
只	只							
他								

ming

nǎ which

shuō

yīng

hái (shì/yú)

fǎ

do (both all)

zhǐ (only)

tā

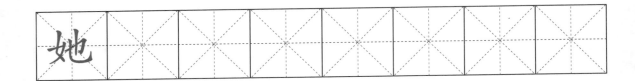

她

练习 liànxí **Exercises**

一、给下面的汉字加上一个偏旁,把它变成另外一个汉字:

Add a radical to each of the following Chinese characters to change them into other characters:

也 ＿＿＿＿＿＿＿＿＿

子 ＿＿＿＿＿＿＿＿＿

不 ＿＿＿＿＿＿＿＿＿   你 ＿＿＿＿＿＿＿＿＿

马 ＿＿＿＿＿＿＿＿＿   门 ＿＿＿＿＿＿＿＿＿

二、写出含有下列偏旁的汉字:

Write Chinese characters containing the following radicals:

亻 （dānrénpáng, person）

讠 （yánzìpáng, speech）

女 （nǚzìpáng, woman）

口 （kǒuzìpáng, mouth）

心 （xīnzìdǐ, heart）

辶 （zǒuzhī, go）

三、补上丢失的笔画:

Supply the missing strokes:

我   老   名   是   都

四、组词:

Form words:

e.g. 学（学习）   学（同学）

学 (　　) 　　　字 (　　) 　　　师 (　　)

同 (　　) 　　　语 (　　) 　　　还 (　　)

五、看拼音写汉字：

Write the Chinese characters represented by the *Pinyin* :

Nǐ jiào shénme míngzi?

Tā shì nǐ lǎoshī háishi nǐ tóngxué?

Tāmen yě xuéxí Hànyǔ.

六、猜一猜下面的句子是什么意思：

Guess the meanings of the following sentences:

你说什么？

你们老师老不老？

我只说汉语，不说法语。

同学们都说她是好老师。

Points about Chinese characters

同音字　Tóngyīnzì　**Homonym**

Characters which are pronounced alike but are different in meaning and appearance like 他 and 她 are called homonyms (tóngyīnzì).

组词　Zǔcí　**Forming words**

When learning a Chinese character you should remember not only the pronunciation and strokes of the character, but also its usage, i.e. what characters it combines with. Forming words is a good way to study and memorize Chinese characters. For example:

"师"shī

—— 什么"师"？　　　Shénme "shī"?　　　which *shī* ?

——"老师"的"师"　　"lǎoshī" de "shī"　　the *shī of lǎoshī* .

Dì-èr Kè

第二课

Lesson Two

汉字

1. 很　9 hěn very

很　很　很　很　很　很　很　很　很

彳　+　艮

◆ 你很好。　我很高兴。　我很喜欢你。

---

2. 高　10 gāo tall, high

高　高　高　高　高　高　高　高　高　高

◆ 他很高，我不高。

高 高 高

a two-story building

3. 兴 6 Ⓑ xìng mood 興

   兴 兴 兴 兴 兴 兴

   高兴

   他很高兴,我不高兴。

4. * 认 4 Ⓑ rèn recognize, know, make out 認

   认 认 认 认

   讠 + 人

   认识

5. * 识 7 Ⓑ shi 識

   识 识 识 识 识 识 识

   讠 + 只

   你认识他吗? 我不认识你。

6. 在 6 zài

   在 在 在 在 在 在

   他在中国工作。

7. * 进 7 jìn enter, come/go in 進

   进 进 进 进 进 进 进

   井 + 辶

   进口

8. * 出 5 chū come/ go out

出 出 出 出 出

出口

A combination of the symbol for a foot and the symbol for a cave-dwelling. 出 suggests a person leaving a dwelling.

---

9. * 公 4 Ⓑ gōng public

公 公 公 公

公司

Note: Pay attention to the difference between 厶 and 公.

---

10. * 司 5 Ⓑ sī

司 司 司 司 司

Note: Pay attention to the difference between 司 and 同.

公司

---

11. 工 3 Ⓑ gōng work

工 工 工

工作 工人 worker

A wood tamper, or mallet.

---

12. 作 7 Ⓑ zuò do

作 作 作 作 作 作

亻 + 乍

工作 work, job

13. * 系 7 xì department (of a university/college)

系 系 系 系 系 系 系 系

◆ 中文系　东亚学系(东亚系)

你在什么系?

14. 可 5 Ⓑ kě may, can

可 可 可 可 可　　可 可 可

◆ 可以　可是 but

15. 以 4 Ⓑ yǐ

以 以 以 以

◆ 可以

16. * 给 9 gěi give, to, for　　給

给 给 给 给 给 给 给 给

纟 + 合

◆ 你给他什么? what will you give him

给他打电话 telephone him

17. 打 5 dǎ hit, strike

打 打 打 打 打

扌 + 丁

Note:the third stroke is from down to up, not from up to down.

◆ 打电话 make a phone call　　他打我。 He hits me.

18. 电 5 diàn electricity 電

电 屯 邑 旦 电

电话　电脑 diànnǎo computer　电视 diànshì TV

电影　diànyǐng movie

19. 话 8 huà speech 話

话 话 话 话 话 话 话 话

讠 + 舌

说话　电话　普通话 *Putonghua*　中国话

20. 的 8 de

的 的 的 的 的 的 的 的

白 + 勺

我的电话号码 my phone number　你的工作 your work / job

21. * 号 5 hào number 號

号 号 号 号 号

号码 一月一号 1st of Jan.

22. * 码 8 Ⓑ mǎ 碼

码 码 码 码 码 码 码 码

石 + 马

号码

23. * 发 5 fā send 發

◈ 发 发 发 发 发

◆ 发电子邮件

24. * 邮 7 Ⓑ yóu post, mail 郵

◈ 邮 邱 邱 邮 邱 邮 邮

◀ 由 + 阝

◆ 邮件

25. * 件 6 Ⓑ jiàn

◈ 件 件 件 件 件 件

◀ 亻 + 牛

◆ 邮件 电子邮件

*   *   *   *

26. 这 7 zhè this 這

◈ 这 这 这 这 这 这 这

◣ 文 + 辶

◆ 这是什么？ 这是我的，不是你的。 It's mine, not yours.

27. 朋 8 Ⓑ péng friend

朋 朋 朋 朋 朋 朋 朋 朋

月 + 月

朋友

A string of cowry shells. Cowry shells were used as both money and jewelry in ancient China. The form of the element 月 derives from 贝 bèi, cowry.

28. 友 4 Ⓑ yǒu friend

友 友 友 友

Graphically, two people's right hands are together, signifying "friends".

Note: pay attention to the difference between 友 and 发.

朋友 友好 friendly

29. 请 10 qǐng please

请 请 请 请 请 请 请 请 请

讠 + 青

请进!

30. 坐 7 zuò sit

坐 坐 坐 坐 坐 坐 坐

人 + 人 + 土

请坐! 我坐这儿,你坐那儿。

31. * 谢 12 xiè thank

   谢 谢 谢 谢 诮 诮 诮 诮 诮 谢 谢

   讠 + 身 + 寸

   ◆ 谢谢!　　　谢谢你!

32. * 喝 12 hē drink

   喝 喝 喝 喝 喝 喝 喝 喝 喝 喝 喝 喝

   口 + 曷

   ◆ 喝茶　喝水
   你喝什么?

33. * 茶 9 chá tea

   茶 茶 茶 茶 茶 茶 茶 茶 茶

   艹 + 人 + 朩

34. 哪 9 Ⓑ na 9

   哪 哪 哪 哪 哪 哪 哪 哪 哪

   口 + 那

   ◆ 哪国人　哪儿

35. 儿 2 Ⓑ ér 兒

   儿 儿

   ◆ 这儿 here　那儿 there　哪儿 where
   你在哪儿? Where are you?

36. * 里 7 Ⓑ lǐ

    里 里 里 里 里 里 里

    这里 = 这儿　　那里 = 那儿　　哪里 = 哪儿

37. * 院 9 Ⓑ yuàn

    院 院 院 院 院 院 院 院 院

    阝　+　完

    学院

38. 怎 9 Ⓑ zěn

    怎 怎 怎 怎 怎 怎 怎 怎 怎

    乍　+　心

    怎么样　　怎么 how, by what means

39. 样 10 Ⓑ yàng

    样 样 样 样 样 样 样 样 样 样

    木　+　羊

    怎么样　　一样 same　　不一样 different

    样儿/样子 appearance, shape　　他什么样儿?

40. 漂 14 Ⓑ piào

    漂 漂 漂 漂 漂 漂 漂 漂 漂 漂 漂 漂

    氵　+　票

    漂亮

41. 亮　9 Ⓑ　liàng

亮 亮 亮 亮 亮 亮 亮 亮 亮

◆ 漂亮　明亮 bright　那儿很亮。

Note: Pay attention to the difference between 亮 and 高.

42. * 喜　12 Ⓑ　xǐ

喜 喜 喜 喜 喜 喜 喜 喜 喜 喜 喜 喜

◆ 喜欢

43. * 欢　6 Ⓑ　huān

欢 欢 欢 欢 欢 欢

又　+　欠

◆ 喜欢
我不喜欢她那样子。 I don't like her manner.

44. 那　6　nà　that

那 那 那 那 那 那

◆ 那是什么？　那儿

Note: The left part of the character 那 is not 月.

45. 男　7　nán　man, male

男 男 男 男 男 男 男

田　+　力

◆ 男朋友　男同学　男老师　我们的老师是男的。

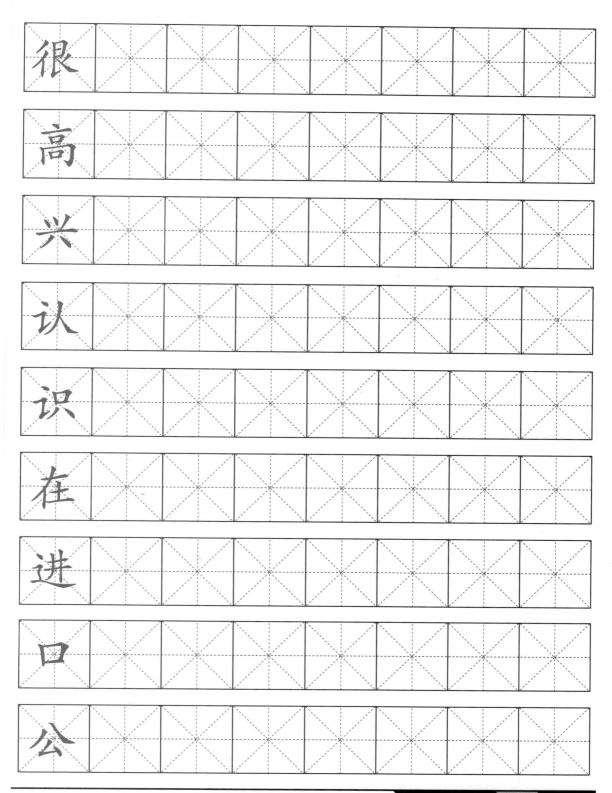

很

高

兴

认

识

在

进

口

公

司

工

作

系

可

以

给

打

电

话

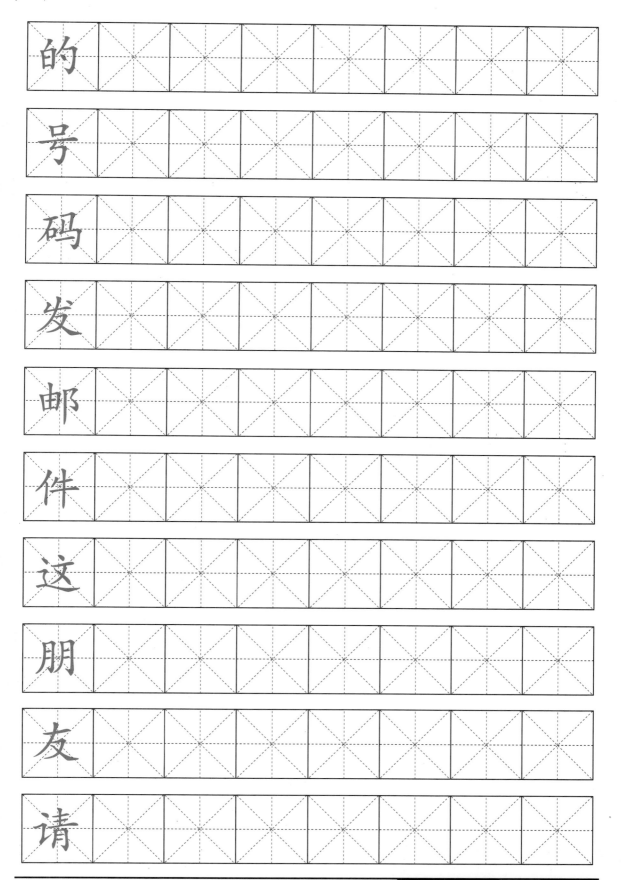

的

号

码

发

邮

件

这 朋

友

请

坐

谢

喝

茶

哪

儿

里

院

怎

样

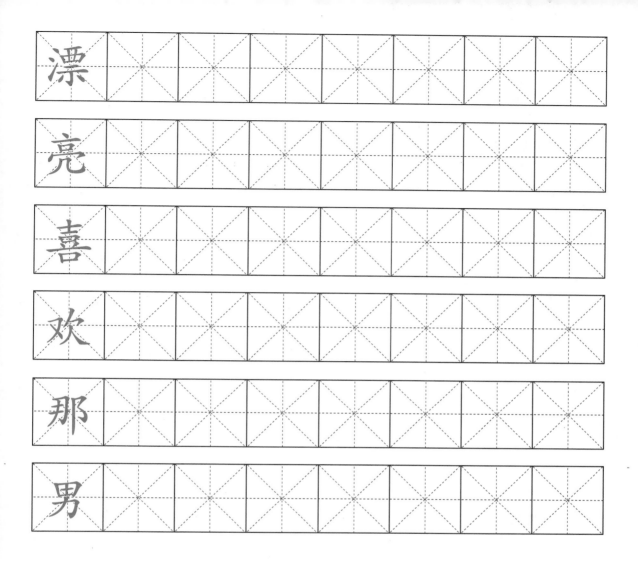

漂

亮

喜

欢

那

男

一、给下面的字加上一个偏旁,把它变成另外一个字:

Add a radical to each of the following characters to change them into other characters:

那　　　文　　　门　　　也

二、写出含有下列偏旁的汉字:

Write Chinese characters containing the following radicals:

扌 (tíshǒupáng,　hand)

心 (xīnzìdǐ,　heart)

木 (mùzìpáng,　tree,　wood)

讠 (yánzìpáng,　speech)

氵 (sāndiǎnshuǐ,　water)

亻 (dānrénpáng,　person)

彳 (shuāngrénpáng,　to pace)

辶 (zǒuzhī,　walk)

三、补上丢失的笔画:

Supply the missing strokes:

很　左　以　可　的　仆　生

四、组词:

Form words:

亮　(　　　)　　　　高　(　　　　)

兴　(　　　)　　　　姓　(　　　　)

打　(　　　)　　　　大　(　　　　)

这　(　　　)　　　　还　(　　　　)

说　(　　　)　　　　话　(　　　　)

学　(　　　)　　　　字　(　　　　)

五、看拼音写汉字:

Write the Chinese characters represented by the *Pinyin*:

Zhè shì wǒ nǚ péngyou.

Nǐ zài nǎr gōngzuò?

Nàr zěnmeyàng?

六、猜一猜下面的句子是什么意思：

Guess the meanings of the following sentences:

你朋友的公司叫什么名字？

我可以在这儿打电话吗？

我说她很漂亮，她很高兴。

你喜欢不喜欢喝中国茶？

Points about Chinese characters

As we have stated before, it often happens that a Chinese character is a word, but sometimes it is only a component of a word. For example, in this text the character 高 itself is a word meaning "high" or "tall", such as 他很高 (he is tall). It can also be combined with 兴 to form the word 高兴 meaning "glad", as in 她很高兴(she is glad). Another example is 大(big), 大学 (university).

In Chinese there is no blank space between words. There is only a space between characters. However, word units clearly exist in the minds of people. Therefore, in the sentence 我很高兴,"高兴" is always regarded as a unit of meaning.

Dì-sān Kè

第三课

Lesson Three

汉字

1. 地　6　dì　ground, earth

地 地 地 地 地 地

土　+　也

Note: Pay attention to the difference between 他 and 地.

地方　什么地方　where　在地上　on the ground

2. 方　4　Ⓑ　fāng

方 方 方 方

地方

3. 个　3　gè　個

个 个 个

一个人　一个地方　两个公司　三个大学

4. 家　10　jiā　home, family

　家 家 家 家 家 家 家 家 家 家

　宀　+　豕

　我家　　在家里　at　home　国家　country

A pig under a roof.

---

5. 有　6　yǒu　have, there be

　有 有 有 有 有 有

　你家有几个人?你有几个中国朋友?

A hand holding a piece of meat.

---

6. 几　2　jǐ　how many　　幾

　几 几

Note: Pay attention to the difference between 儿 and 几.

　几个人

---

7. 爸　8　bà　father

　爸 爸 爸 爸 爸 爸 爸 爸

　父　+　巴

　爸爸

---

8. 和　8　hé　and

　和 和 和 和 和 和 和 和

　禾　+　口

　你和我　　这儿和那儿　　学生和老师　　小学、中学和大学

9. 太 4 ⑧ tài

　　﨎 太 大 大 太

　　◈ 你太太　your wife

---

10. * 孩 9 ⑧ hái　child

　　﨎 孩 孩 孩 孩 孩 孩 孩 孩 孩

　　﨏 孑 ＋ 亥

　　◈ 孩子　小孩子　男孩儿　女孩儿

---

11. 多 6 duō　many, much, a lot of

　　﨎 多 夕 夕 多 多 多

　　﨑 夕 ＋ 夕

Two pieces of meat.

Note: When the upper part of 名 is reduplicated it becomes 多.

　　◈ 多少　我家有很多人。　我家人很多。
　　　你多大？

---

12. 两 7 liǎng　two　兩

　　﨎 两 两 两 两 两 两 两

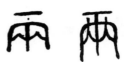

Note:　There are two 人 inside.

　　◈ 两个人

---

13. 岁 6 suì　age　歲

　　﨎 岁 岁 岁 岁 岁 岁

⊻ 山 + 夕

◆ 他三十岁。

---

14. 爱 10 ài love 爱

⊭ 爱 爱 爱 爱 爱 爱 爱 爱 爱 爱

⊻ ⺫ + 冖 + 友

◆ 可爱　爱人 spouse

我爱她，她不爱我。

---

15. * 吧 7 ba

⊭ 吧 吧 吧 吧 吧 吧 吧

⋈ 口 + 巴

◆ 她很可爱吧？你是中国人吧？

*   *   *   *

---

16. 校 10 Ⓑ xiào school

⊭ 校 校 校 校 校 校 校 校 校 校

⋈ 木 + 交

◆ 学校

---

17. 少 4 shǎo few, little

⊭ 少 少 少 少

◆ 多少

我家有不少人。　我家人很少。

Note: Pay attention to the difference between 小 and 少.

---

18. 生　5　Ⓑ　shēng　student

⋇ 生　生　生　生　生

◆ 学生　大学生 university student　男生　女生

中学生 middle school student　　小学生 pupil

---

19. 想　13　xiǎng　think, want to do sth.

⋇ 想 想 想 想 想 想 想 想 想 想 想 想 想

⋇ 木　＋　目　＋　心

◆ 让我想一下。　我想去中国。

我不想在那个公司工作。

Note: There is a 心 below. Ancient people thought people think with their 心.

20.* 概　13　Ⓑ　gài

⋇ 概 概 概 概 概 概 概 概 概 概 概 概 概

⋇ 木　＋　既

◆ 大概　maybe, about

21. 万　3　wàn　ten thousand　萬

◗ 万　万　万

◆ 一万个学生

Note: If you add a *Dian* to 万, it becomes 方 of 地方.

---

22. 没　7　méi　not have

◗ 没 没 没 没 没 没 没

◗ 氵　+　几　+　又

◆ 没有

---

23. 千　3　qiān　thousand

◗ 千　千　千

Note: The first stroke is Piě , not Héng .

◆ 一万三千

---

24. 去　5　qù　go

◗ 去　去　去　去　去

◆ 你想去哪儿？

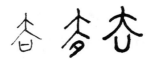

---

25. 为　4　wèi　for　爲

◗ 为　为　为　为

◆ 你为什么不想在那个公司工作？

26. 分   4   fēn   branch

     分   分   分   分   

     八   +   刀

     分校   分公司

---

27. 公   4   Ⓑ   gōng

     公   公   公   公

     八   +   厶

Note: Pay attention to the difference between 公 and the 厶 of 什么.

     公司

28.* 板   8   Ⓑ   bǎn

     板 板 板 板 板 板 板 板

     木   +   反

     老板   黑板 hēibǎn   blackboard

---

29. 让   5   ràng   let   讓

     让   让   让   让   让

     讠   +   上

     他不让我去。He doesn't let me go there.

---

30. 百   6   bǎi   hundred

     百 百 百 百 百 百

     一万三千五百

31. 因 6 Ⓑ yīn reason, cause

因 因 因 因 因 因

◆ 因为

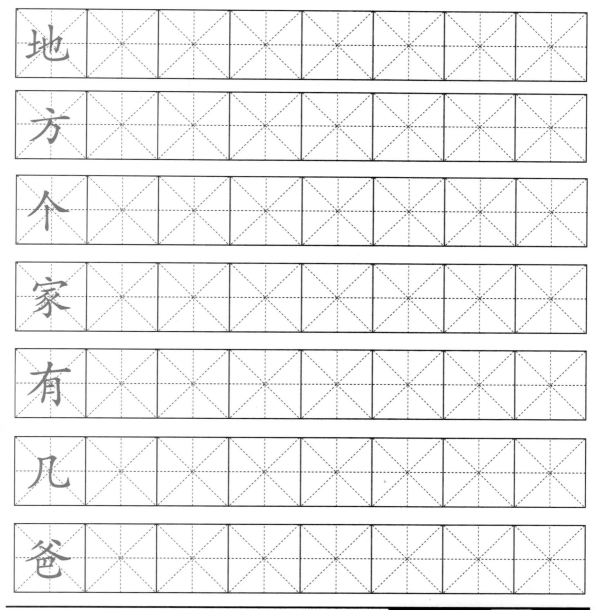

地

方

个

家

有

几

爸

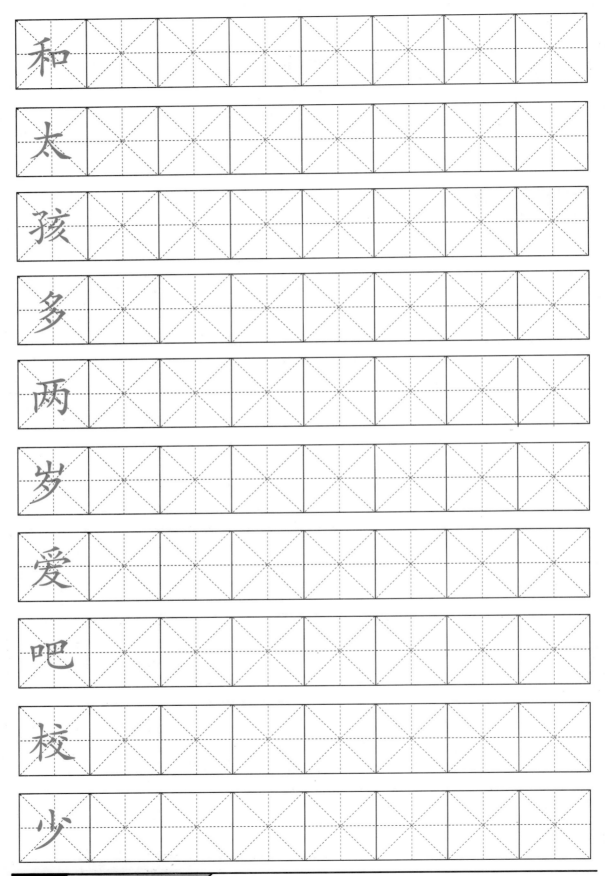

和

太

孩

多

两

岁

爱

吧

校

少

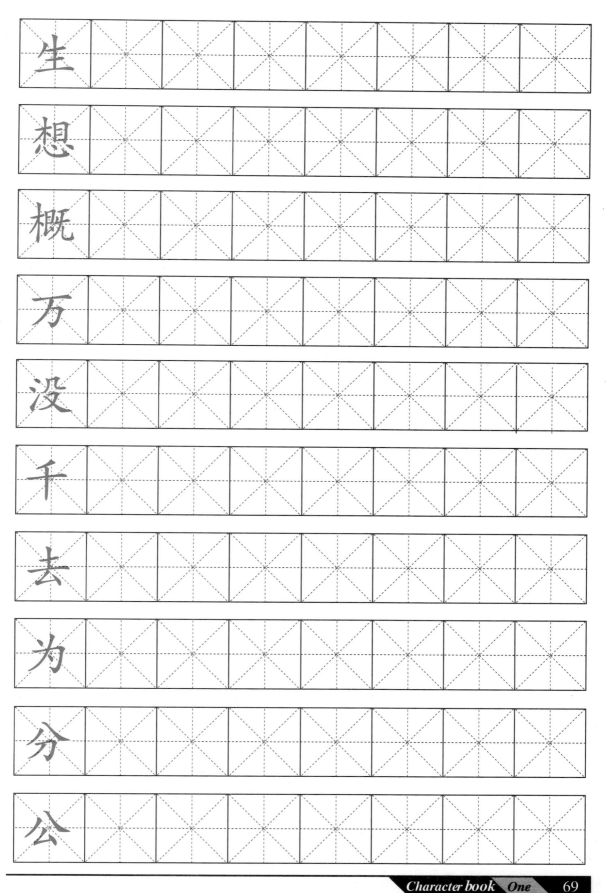

生

想

概

万

没

千

去

为

分

公

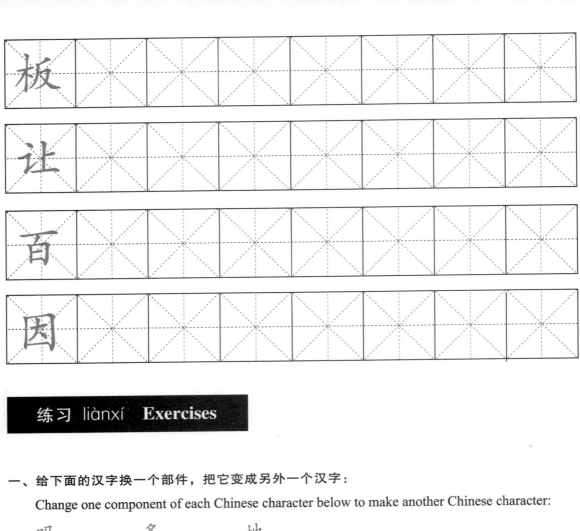

板

让

百

因

一、给下面的汉字换一个部件，把它变成另外一个汉字：

Change one component of each Chinese character below to make another Chinese character:

吗　　　多　　　地

二、比较下列汉字，并注上拼音：

Give the *Pinyin* for these pairs of similar characters.

方（　　）　万（　　）　家（　　）　字（　　）

名（　　）　岁（　　）　小（　　）　少（　　）

姓（　　）　生（　　）　人（　　）　个（　　）

三、补上丢失的笔画：

Supply the missing strokes:

为　爱　爸　冂　家　校　想

四、组词:

Form words:

地 (   )   爱 (   )

校 (   )   生 (   )

没 (   )   多 (   )

因 (   )

五、看拼音写汉字:

Write the Chinese characters represented by the *Pinxin*:

Nǐ tàitài shì shénme dìfang rén?

Ní wèi shénme xiǎng xuéxí Hànyǔ?

Wǒmen xuéxiào yǒu yì qiān sān bǎi gè xuésheng.

六、猜一猜下面的句子是什么意思:

Guess the meanings of the following sentences:

孩子很可爱,爸爸、妈妈很爱她。

他们国家人口不多,只有一千万。

他很不高兴,因为他很想去那个地方工作,可是公司老板不让他去。

Points about Chinese characters

At present, the major Chinese character input systems use keyboard input, which can be subdivided into two input techniques: one is *pinyin* input (Romanized spelling based on a character's pronunciation) and the other is character code input (keyboard-based codes representing Chinese character components or strokes). The *pinyin* input method allows input based on a character's pronunciation spelled in *Hanyu Pinyin*, which is automatically converted into Chinese characters by the computer.

People who do not speak standard Mandarin or who are not familiar with the *pinyin* system will prefer a character code input method. The code input method selects Chinese characters by using Arabic numerals or letters of the alphabet as codes. One types in the codes, which the computer changes into characters. There must be several hundred systems for character codes, but the most widely used code system on the market today is the "five-stroke" input method.

Besides the proliferation of keyboard input methods, there has been rapid development in the field of automatic character shape recognition and voice recognition technologies. At present there are already software and peripheral products on the market that allow the computer to "recognize" a person's handwriting or voice, and convert either into Chinese characters.

Dì-sì Kè

第四课

Lesson Four

汉字

1. 图   8   tú   picture   圖

⿻   图   图 图 图 图 图 图 图

⿴   囗   +   冬

◆   一张图   地图

2. 张   7   zhāng   張

⿻   张 张 张 张 张 张 张

⿻   弓   +   长

◆   一张地图   他姓张。

3. 英   8   Ⓑ   yīng

⿻   英 英 英 英 英 英 英 英

⿱   艹   +   央

◆   英国   英语   英文

4. 看　9　kàn　look

看 看 看 看 看 看 看 看 看　

◆ 看一下　看朋友　看地图　看词典　看书

5. 行　6　xíng

行 行 行 行 行 行

彳 ＋ 丁

◆ 行。　不行。

Diagram of a crossroad.

6. 要　9　yào　want

要 要 要 要 要 要 要 要 要

西 ＋ 女

◆ 你要什么？　你要干什么？

7. 给　9　gěi　give to; for　給

给 给 给 给 给 给 给 给

纟 ＋ 合

◆ 给我打电话 他给我一张地图。

8. 干　3　gàn　do　幹

干 干 干

Note: Pay attention to the difference between 千 and 干.

◆ 干什么

9. 玩　8　wán　play

　　玩 玩 玩　玩 玩 玩 玩 玩

　　王 ＋ 元

　◆ 我们去玩儿。　他不喜欢上课,只喜欢玩儿。

10. 知　8　Ⓑ　zhī

　　知 知 知 知 知 知 知 知

　　矢 ＋ 口

　◆ 知道　不知道

11. 道　12　Ⓑ　dào

　　道 道 道 道 道 道 道 道 道 道 道 道

　　首 ＋ 辶

　◆ 知道

12. 比　4　bǐ　than

　　比 比 比 比

　◆ 这个比那个好。 This one is better than that one.

比比 比比 比比

Two persons standing,　one in front of the other.

13. 较　10　Ⓑ　jiào　较

　　较 较 较 较 较 较 较 较 较 较

　　车 ＋ 交

　◆ 比较　这个比较好,那个非常好。

　　请比较一下这两个词。 Please compare the two words.

14. 真　10　zhēn　really, true

真 真 真 真 真 真 真 真 真 真

◆ 真的吗？ Really?　真漂亮！ It's so beautiful!

15. 意　13　Ⓑ　yì

意 意 意 意 意 意 意 意 意 意 意 意

✕ 立　＋　日　＋　心

◆ 意思

16. 思　9　Ⓑ　sī

思 思 思 思 思 思 思 思 思

✕ 田　＋　心

◆ 意思　你是什么意思？ What do you mean?

他很有意思。He is interesting.

17. 龙　5　lóng　dragon　　　龍

龙 龙 龙 龙 龙

18. 山　3　shān　mountain, hill

山 山 山

A mountain with three peaks.

◆ 小山　大山　高山　他在山上，我在山下。

19. 词　7　cí　word　詞

　　⋈ 词　词　词　词　词　词　词

　　⋈ 讠 ＋ 司

　　◆ 一个词 a word　生词 new word　词典 dictionary

　　　词语 words and expressions

　　Note: The right part is 司 of 公司.

20.* 典　8　Ⓑ　diǎn

　　⋈ 典　典　典　典　典　典　典　典

　　◆ 词典　字典

---

21. 本　5　běn

　　⋈ 本　木　木　木　本

　　◆ 一本书　一本词典　一个本子

The roots of a tree indicated by an additional short stroke near the base of the character for 木(mù), tree.

---

22. 谁　10　shuí, shéi　who　誰

　　⋈ 谁　谁　谁　谁　谁　谁　谁　谁　谁

　　⋈ 讠 ＋ 亻 ＋ 主

　　◆ 他是谁?　这是谁的书?

---

23. 问　6　wèn　ask　問

　　⋈ 问　问　问　问　问　问

　　✕ 门 ＋ 口

　　◆ 请问　他问我

24. 对　5　duì　right, correct, yes　　對

　　对　对　对　对　对

　　又　+　寸

　　对不对？　不对。

---

25. 非　8　Ⓑ　fēi

　　非　非　非　非　非　非　非　非

　　非常

---

26. 常　11　cháng

　　常　常　常　常　常　常　常　常　常　常　常

　　⺌　+　口　+　巾

　　非常　　常常　often

---

27. 用　5　yòng　use

　　用　用　用　用　用

　　你用不用词典？

　　汉语很有用　这本词典没(有)用(useless)

　　老板说他真没用。

---

28. 能　10　néng　can

　　能　能　能　能　能　能　能　能　能　能

　　你能不能来？

29. * 当 6 Ⓑ dāng 當

当 当 当 当 当 当

◆ 当然　当代 dāngdài　contemporary

---

30. * 然 12 Ⓑ rán

然 然 然 然 然 然 然 然 然 然 然 然

夕 ＋ 犬 ＋ 灬

Its original meaning was "burn".

◆ 当然

---

31. 书 4 shū book 書

书 书 书 书

◆ 一本书　看书

---

32. * 笔 10 bǐ pen 筆

笔 笔 笔 笔 笔 笔 笔 笔 笔 笔

竹 ＋ 毛

◆ 这支笔你用不用？

---

33. * 支 4 zhī

支 支 支 支

◆ 一支笔

34.* 教　11　Ⓑ　jiào teaching; jiāo to teach

教 教 教 教 教 教 教 教 教 教

耂 ＋ 子 ＋ 攵

教室　他教我们汉语。

35.* 室　9　Ⓑ　shì　room

室 室 室 室 室 室 室 室 室

宀 ＋ 至

教室　工作室

36. 课　10　kè lesson

课 课 课 课 课 课 课 课 课 课

讠 ＋ 果

上课　下课　有课　汉语课　　课本 textbook　　课文 text

写汉字

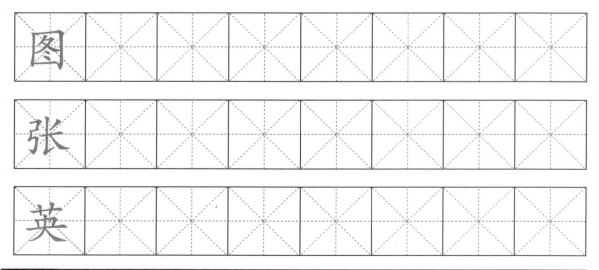

图

张

英

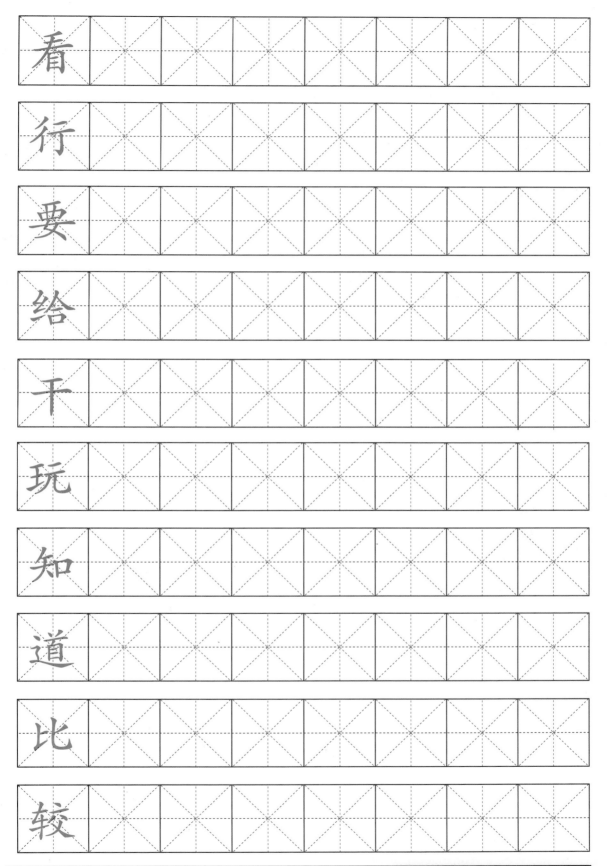

看

行

要

给

干

玩

知

道

比

较

真

意

思

龙

山

词

典

本

谁

问

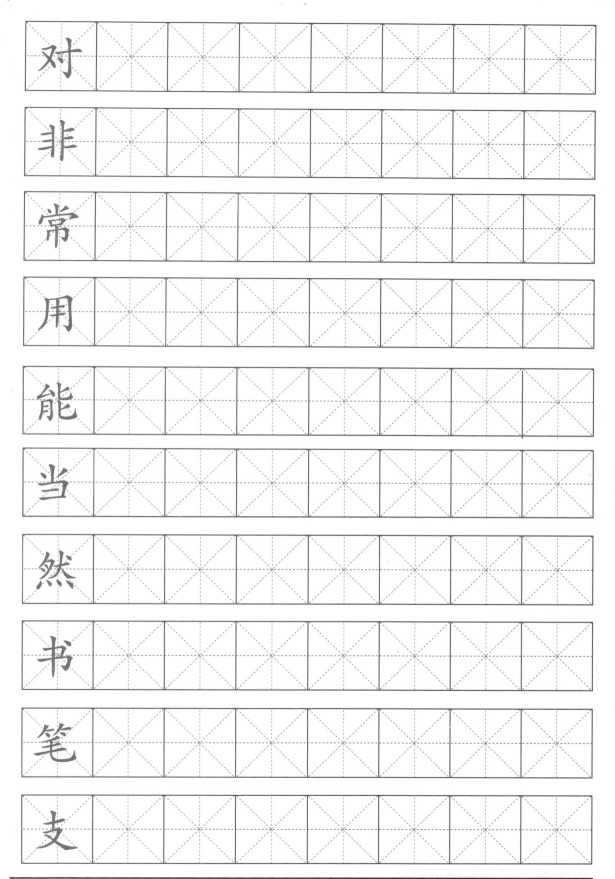

对

非

常

用

能

当

然

书

笔

支

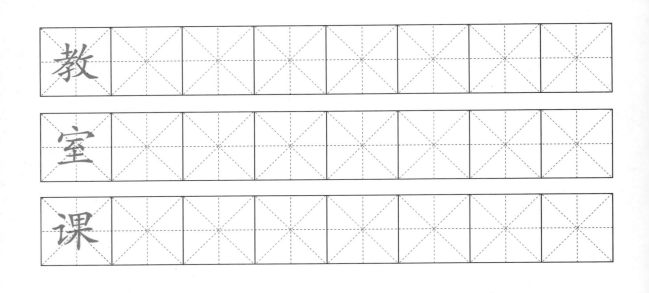

一、比较下列汉字，并注上拼音：

Give the *Pinyin* for these pairs of similar characters:

干（　　）　　千（　　）　　同（　　）　　词（　　）

木（　　）　　本（　　）　　较（　　）　　校（　　）

问（　　）　　门（　　）

二、补上丢失的笔画：

Supply the missing strokes:

图　妾　看　真　能　书

三、写出含有下列偏旁的汉字：

Write Chinese characters containing the following radicals:

囗（kǒuzìkuāng, enclosuer）

王（wángzìpáng, jade）

艹（cǎozìtóu, grass）

讠（yánzìpáng, speech）

辶（zǒuzhī, walk）

彳 (shuāngrénpáng, go pace)

四、组词：

Form words:

常（　　　　　　）　　　比（　　　　　　）

图（　　　　　　）　　　用（　　　　　　）

道（　　　　　　）　　　课（　　　　　　）

五、看拼音写汉字：

Write the Chinese characters represented by the *Pinyin*：

Tā gěi wǒ yì zhāng dìtú.

Néng bu néng gěi wǒ kàn yíxia?

Zhè běn shū fēicháng yǒuyòng.

六、猜一猜下面的句子是什么意思：

Guess the meanings of the following sentences:

你不问，他不说。

谁知道他想要干什么！

请你比较一下这两本书，哪一本有意思？

这本书没有意思，可是非常有用；那本书非常有意思，可是没有用。

Points about Chinese characters

There is a difference between a character dictionary (zìdiǎn) and a word dictionary (cídiǎn). Character dictionaries mainly gloss characters while word dictionaries mainly explain words. Word dictionaries can also function as character dictionaries, because they are arranged in the order of principal characters　(usually the first character of a word).　The principal character appears first, followed by words that begin with it. Most word dictionaries are arranged alphabetically according to the *pinyin* spelling of words and usually contain a radical index,　too.　Some word dictionaries are arranged according to the radicals of the principal characters but also contain a *pinyin* index.

Dì-wǔ Kè

第五课

Lesson Five

汉 字

1. 姐　8　jiě　elder sister

　　姐 姐 姐 姐 姐 姐 姐 姐

　　女　+　且

　　小姐　姐姐 elder sister

2. 会　6　huì　can, know how to　會

　　会 会 会 会 会 会

　　你会不会说汉语?

3. 点　9　diǎn　drop, point, dot; select, choose　點

　　点 点 点 点 点 点 点 点 点

　　一点儿　点菜 choose dishes from a menu

4. 先　6　xiān　first

A foot above a person, indicating one person going ahead of another.

先 先 先 先 先 先

先生　张先生　我(的)先生　my husband

您先请。　You first please.　我先去。　I'll go first.

---

5. 买　6　mǎi　buy　買

买 买 买 买 买 买

一 ＋ 头

买东西

6.* 衬　8　Ⓑ　chèn　襯

衬 衬 衬 衬 衬 衬 衬 衬

衤 ＋ 寸

衬衫

7.* 衫　8　Ⓑ　shān

衫 衫 衫 衫 衫 衫 衫 衫

衤 ＋ 彡

衬衫

---

8. 白　5　bái　white

白 白 白 白 白

我要白的　白衬衫

A burning candle.

9. 钱 10 qián money 錢

    钱 钱 钱 钱 钱 钱 钱 钱 钱 钱

    钅 + 戋

    多少钱　他很有钱。我没有钱。

---

10. * 块 7 kuài 塊

    块 块 块 块 块 块 块

    土 + 夬

    三块钱

---

11. 元 4 yuán

    元 元 元 元

    三元钱

---

12. 了 2 le

    了 了

    太好了！

---

13. 贵 9 guì expensive, highly valued, honored 貴

    贵 贵 贵 贵 贵 贵 贵 贵 贵

    中 + 一 + 贝

    这件衬衫很贵。　您贵姓？

14. 红 6 hóng red 红

　　红 红 红 红 红 红

　　纟 ＋ 工

　　我要红的　红衬衫

15. 便 9 ⑧ pián

　　便 便 便 便 便 便 便 便 便

　　亻 ＋ 更

　　便宜

16. 宜 8 ⑧ yí

　　宜 宜 宜 宜 宜 宜 宜 宜

　　宀 ＋ 且

　　那儿的东西很便宜。

17.* 条 7 tiáo 條

　　条 条 条 条 条 条 条

　　夂 ＋ 木

　　一条裤子　一条河

18.* 裤 12 ⑧ kù 裤

　　裤 裤 裤 裤 裤 裤 裤 裤 裤 裤 裤 裤

　　衤 ＋ 库

　　裤子

19.* 试 8 shì 試

試 试 试 试 试 试 试 试

讠 + 式

◆ 让我试一试。/我来试一试。Let me try.

20. 来 7 lái come 来

来 来 来 来 来 来 来

◆ 来这儿

Its original meaning was "wheat". Later it was loaned for use in 来(come).

21. 饭 7 fàn steamed rice 飯

饭 饭 饭 饭 饭 饭 饭

饣 + 反

◆ 米饭　饭菜　饭店　吃饭

22. 店 8 diàn shop

店 店 店 店 店 店 店 店

广 + 占

◆ 书店　饭店　一个店 / 一家店　在店里

23. 最 12 zuì the most

最 最 最 最 最 最 最 最 最 最 最

曰 + 取

◆ 最好　最漂亮　最有意思

24. 吃　6　chī　eat

吃　吃　吃　吃　吃　吃

口　+　乞

吃饭　好吃

25.*　菜　11　cài　dish

菜　菜　菜　菜　菜　菜　菜　菜　菜　菜　菜

艹　+　采

买菜　吃菜　中国菜

26.*　糖　16　táng　sugar

糖　糖　糖　糖　糖　糖　糖　糖　糖　糖　糖　糖　糖　糖

米　+　唐

喜欢吃糖　糖是甜(tián, sweet)的。

27.*　醋　15　cù　vinegar

醋　醋　醋　醋　醋　醋　醋　醋　醋　醋　醋　醋　醋　醋　醋

酉　+　昔

吃醋　be jealous (usually of a rival in love)

醋是酸的。

28.　鱼　8　yú　fish　魚

鱼　鱼　鱼　鱼　鱼　鱼　鱼　鱼

一条鱼

92　当代中文

29.* 酸　14　suān　sour

　　　酸酸酸酸酸 酸酸酸 酸酸酸酸酸酸

　　　酉　+　夋

　◆ 这个菜比较酸。

30.* 辣　14　là　peppery, hot

　　　辣辣辣 辣辣 辣 辣辣 辣 辣 辣 辣 辣辣

　　　辛　+　束

　◆ 这个菜比较辣。

31.* 汤　6　tāng　soup

　　　汤 汤 汤　汤 汤 汤

　　　氵　+　易

　◆ 喝汤　酸辣汤

---

32. 牛　4　niú　cow, cattle, ox

　　　牛 牛 牛 牛

　◆ 一头牛　牛肉

The front view of an ox's head with horns.

---

33. 肉　6　ròu　meat

　　　肉 肉 肉 肉 肉 肉

　◆ 牛肉　鱼肉

A drawing of a piece of meat.

34.* 烧 10 shāo cook 燒

烧 烧 烧 烧 烧 烧 烧 烧 烧 烧

火 + 尧

红烧 烧菜 烧饭 烧水

35. 米 6 mǐ rice

米 米 米 米 米 米

A scattered paddy.

大米 米饭

36.* 饺 9 jiǎo 餃

饺 饺 饺 饺 饺 饺 饺 饺 饺

饣 + 交

水饺 饺子

37. 等 12 děng wait

等 等 等 等 等 等 等 等 等 等 等 等

⺮ + 寺

请等一下。 我等你。

38. 东 5 Ⓑ dōng east 東

东 东 东 东 东

东西 东方 the East, the Orient 东方人

39. 西 6 Ⓑ xī west

西 西 西 西 西 西

东西 (here 西 is in neural tone)

西方 the West 西方人

40. 商 11 Ⓑ shāng trade, business

商 商 商 商 商 商 商 商 商 商

商店

41. 卖 8 mài sell 賣

卖 卖 卖 卖 卖 卖 卖 卖

土 + 头

卖东西

42. 衣 6 Ⓑ yī clothes

衣 衣 衣 衣 衣 衣

衣服

43. 服 8 Ⓑ fú clothes

服 服 服 服 服 服 服 服

月 + 艮

衣服

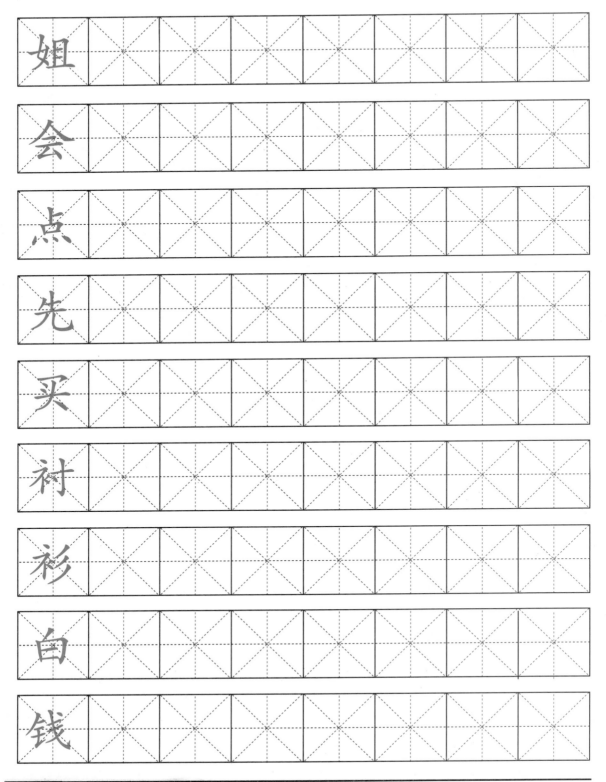

姐

会

点

先

买

衬

衫

白

钱

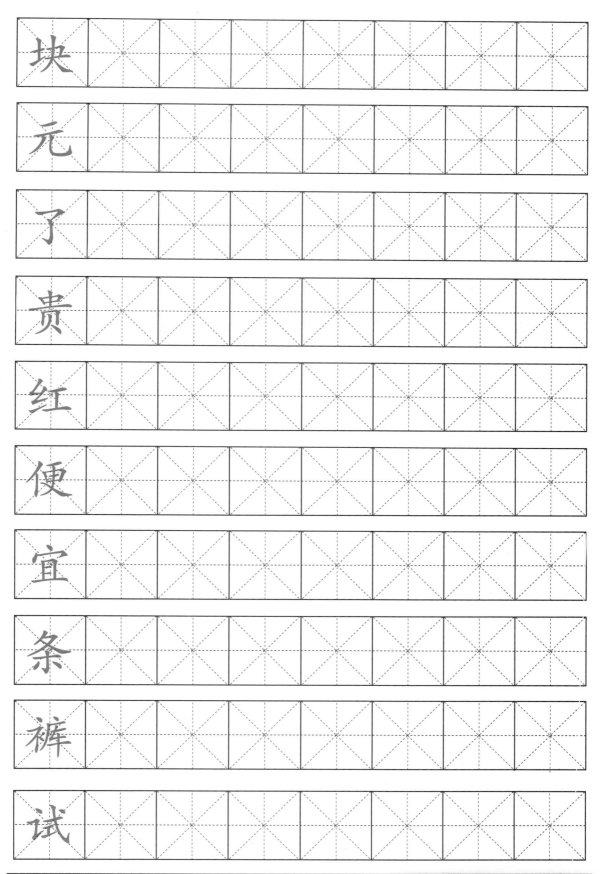

块
元
了
贵
红
便
宜
条
裤
试

来
饭
店
最
吃
菜
糖
醋
鱼
酸

辣

汤

牛

肉

烧

米

饺

等

东

西

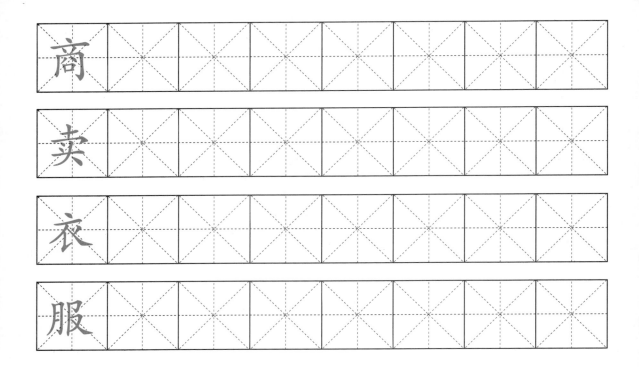

商

卖

衣

服

一、比较下列汉字,并注上拼音:

Give the *Pinyin* for these pairs of similar characters.

百 (）   白 (）   子 (）   了 (）

木 (）   本 (）   米 (）   来 (）

牛 (）   生 (）   西 (）   四 (）

点 (）   店 (）   买 (）   卖 (）

二、补上丢失的笔画:

Supply the missing strokes:

使　宜　车　最　内　等　钱

三、写出含有下列偏旁的汉字:

Write Chinese characters containing the following radicals:

口（kǒuzìpáng，　mouth）

钅 (jīnzìpáng, metal)

饣 (shízìpáng, eat, food)

纟 (jiǎosīpáng, silk)

⺮ (zhúzìtóu, bamboo)

亻 (dānrénpáng, person)

四、组词：

Form words:

肉 (   )   宜 (   )

东 (   )   姐 (   )

店 (   )   先 (   )

衣 (   )

五、看拼音写汉字：

Write the Chinese characters represented by the *Pinyin*：

Nǐ yào mǎi shénme dōngxi?

Wǒ xiǎng chī niúròu hé mǐfàn.

Tài guì le! Yǒu méiyǒu piányi yìdiǎnr de?

六、猜一猜下面的句子是什么意思：

Guess the meanings of the following sentences:

请等一下，让我想一想。

这家饭店的菜非常好吃，汤也很好喝。

便宜的东西不好，好的东西不便宜，你说是不是？

她家里有很多衣服，可是她说她没有衣服。她喜欢商店里的衣服，不喜欢家里的衣服。

Points about Chinese characters

Most Chinese characters are picto-phonetic. Usually, the picto-radical is on the left and indicates the character's category of meaning,   while the phonetic radical is on the right and suggests its pronunciation. For example, in the character 饭, the 饣 shízìpáng means that the character is related to food, and 反 indicates the pronunciation (only roughly, for 反 is in the third tone, while 饭 is fourth tone). Language and written characters have changed constantly throughout history. For example, the radical of the character 纟jiǎosī páng originally referred to the color of silk products, but now 红 is used for the red color of all kinds of objects ;   the right side of the character 工 resembles the sound of 红 only in its final. The radical of 钱 is 钅(jīnzìpáng) (gold, metal), for ancient coins were made of metal. The radical 女 (nǚzìpáng)of 姓 may refer to an earlier matrilineal society.

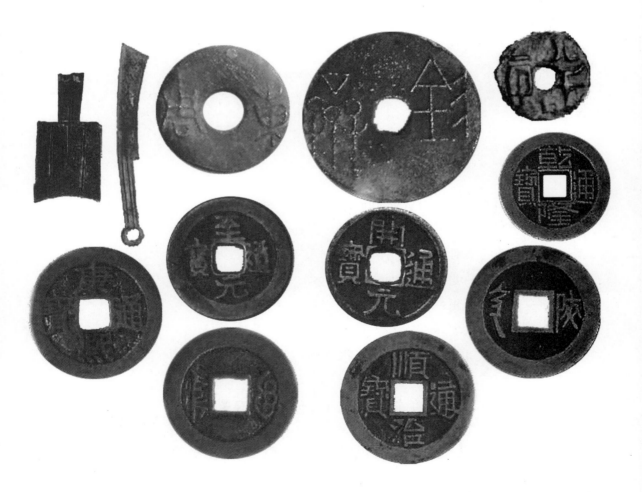

Dì-liù Kè

第六课

Lesson Six

汉 字

1. 星 9 Ⓑ xīng star

星 星 星 星 星 星 星 星 星

曰 + 生

星期 星星 xīngxing star

2. 期 12 Ⓑ qī period

期 期 期 期 期 其 其 期 期 期 期 期

其 + 月

星期 week 学期 semester

3.* 算 14 suàn calculate

算 算 算 算 算 算 算 算 算 算 算 算 算

竹 + 目 + 廾

打算 算一算多少钱。

4. 晚 11 wǎn late

晚 晚 晚 晚 晚 晚 晚 晚 晚 晚 晚

日 ＋ 免

晚上　晚饭 supper　太晚了 It's too late.

他来晚了。He came late.

5. 约 6 yuē to date 約

约 约 约 约 约 约

纟 ＋ 勺

约会　约她在咖啡馆见面

6. 里 7 lǐ in, inside 裏

里 里 里 里 里 里 里

这里　那里　哪里　家里　学校里　商店里　教室里

7. 休 6 ⑧ xiū

休 休 休 休 休 休

亻 ＋ 木

休息

A person resting against a tree.

8. 息 10 ⑧ xī

息 息 息 息 息 息 息 息 息 息

自 ＋ 心

休息

9. 球　11　qiú　ball

球　球　球　球　球　球　球　球　球　球　球

王　+　求

打球　地球　the earth

10. 跟　13　gēn　with, and

跟　跟　跟　跟　跟　跟　跟　跟　跟　跟　跟　跟　跟

𧾷　+　艮

跟他一起去　我跟我同学说汉语。你跟他是什么关系？
我跟他们没有关系。

11. 起　10　Ⓑ　qǐ

起　起　起　起　起　起　起　起　起　起

走　+　己

Note: The seventh stroke is a bit longer to prop up 己.

一起

12.* 视　8　Ⓑ　shì　look　视

视　视　视　视　视　视　视　视

礻　+　见

Note: the left part is different from the left part of 衬衫. The left part of 视 is 礻, not 衤.

电视

13.* 位　7　wèi

位 位 位 位 位 位 位

亻　+　立

一位朋友

14. 事　8　shì　thing (to do)

事 事 事 事 事

事 事 事

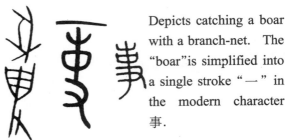

Depicts catching a boar with a branch-net. The "boar" is simplified into a single stroke "一" in the modern character 事.

一件事儿　有事儿　做事儿

同事　colleague

15.* 咖　8　Ⓑ　kā

咖 咖 咖 叻 咖 咖 咖 咖

口　+　加

咖啡

16.* 啡　11　Ⓑ　fēi

啡 啡 啡 啡 啡 啡 啡 啡 啡 啡 啡

口　+　非

咖啡

17. 时　7　Ⓑ　shí　時

时 时 时 时 时 时 时

日　+　寸

时候

18. 候 10 Ⓑ hòu

候 候 候 候 候 候 候 候 候 候

亻 + ユ + ㄡ

什么时候　有的时候 sometimes　这个时候　this moment

那个时候　that moment

他太太做饭的时候，他看电视。

He watches TV when his wife is making the dinner.

(…的时候，when)

19. 今 4 Ⓑ jīn

今 今 今 今

今天

20. 忙 6 máng busy

忙 忙 忙 忙 忙 忙

忄 + 亡

我今天很忙。

21. 做 11 zuò do

做 做 做 做 做 做 做 做 做 做 做

亻 + 故

你做什么工作？

在你们家谁做饭？

他在家里不做事儿。

22. * 功　5　Ⓑ　gōng

功 功 功 功 功

工　＋　力

功课　用功　hardworking (in study)

---

23. 关　6　Ⓑ　guān

关 关 关 关 关 关

关系

---

24. 系　7　Ⓑ　xì

系 系 系 系 系 系 系

关系　relation

东亚(学)系　Department of East Asian Studies

---

25. 空　8　kòng

空 空 空 空 空 空 空 空

穴　＋　工

有空儿　没空儿

---

26. 钟　9　zhōng　bell, clock　　鐘

钟 钟 钟 钟 钟 钟 钲 钲 钟

钅　＋　中

三点钟

27. 半　5　bàn　half

半 半 半 半 半

◆ 一半　half　三点半　半张地图　半天　half a day

28. 见　4　jiàn　see　見

见 见 见 见

Drawing of a man who opens his eyes to see.

◆ 见面　再见　我明天去见老师。

明天见！　一会儿见！ See you later.

29. 面　9　miàn　face, surface; flour, noodles

面 面 面 面 面 面 面 面 面

◆ 见面　　面条 noodles

30. * 刻　8　kè　quarter (of an hour)

刻 刻 刻 刻 刻 刻 刻 刻

亥　＋　刂

◆ 一点三刻

31. * 接　11　jiē

接 接 接 接 接 接 接 接 接 接

扌　＋　妾

◆ 接人　接电话 answer the phone

32. 再　6　zài　again

再 再 冉 冄 再 再

再见！　明天再来。　我想再去。

33. 现　8　Ⓑ　xiàn　now　现

现 现 现 现 现 现 现 现

王　+　见

现在

34. 分　4　fēn　branch, minute, cent

分 分 分 分

分公司　三点四十分　五块三毛四分

35. 早　6　zǎo　early

早 早 早 早 早 早

日　+　十

早上　太早了！　It's too early.　早上好！　Good morning.

早饭　breakfast

36. 午　4　Ⓑ　wǔ

午 午 午 午

Note: pay attention to the difference between "午" and "牛".

上午　下午　中午　noon　午饭　lunch

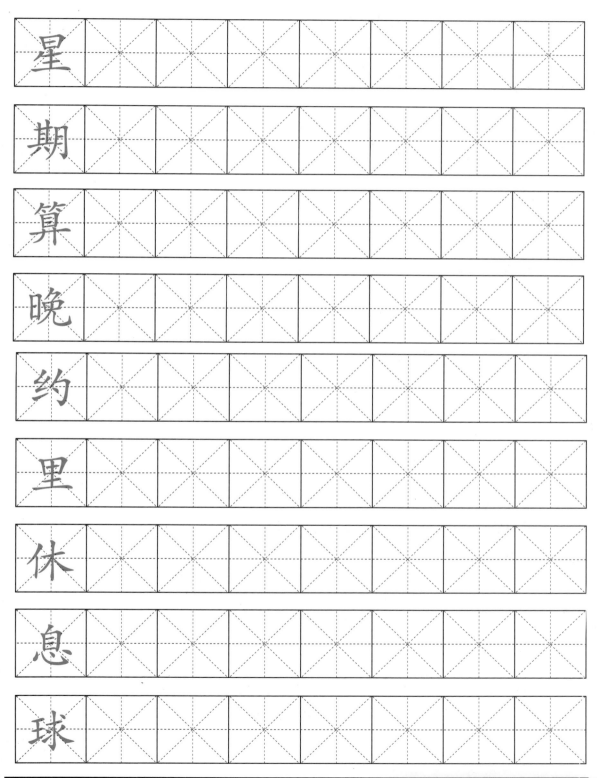

星

期

算

晚

约

里

休

息

球

跟

起

视

位

事

咖

啡

时

候

今

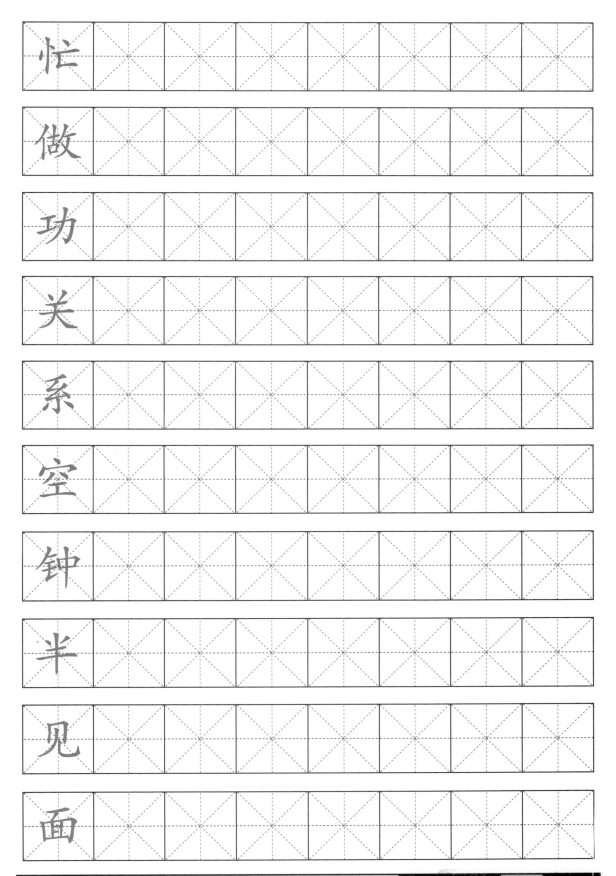

忙

做

功

关

系

空

钟

半

见

面

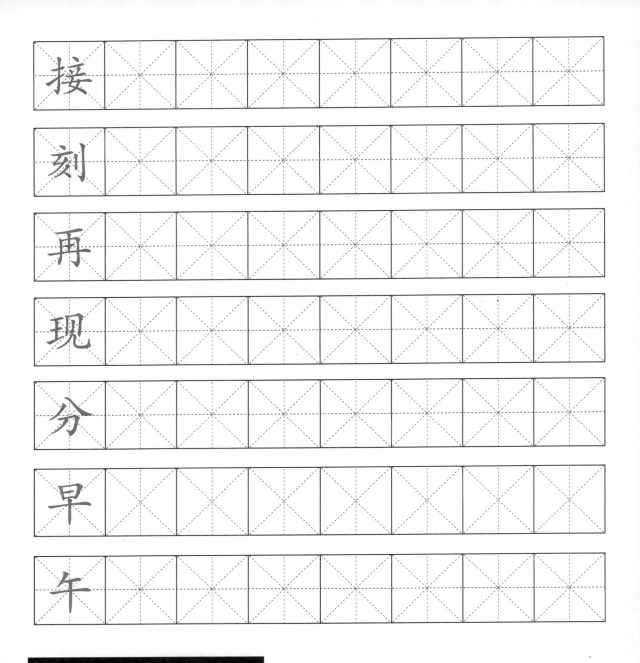

接

刻

再

现

分

早

午

一、比较下列汉字，并注上拼音：

Give the *Pinyin* for these pairs of similar characters.

红（　　） 约（　　） 来（　　） 半（　　）

今（　　） 会（　　） 午（　　） 牛（　　）

姓（　　） 星（　　） 很（　　） 跟（　　）

二、写出含有下列偏旁的汉字:
Write Chinese characters containing the following radicals:

忄 (shùxīnpáng, heart)

王 (wángzìpáng, jade)

足 (zúzìpáng, foot)

日 (rìzìpáng, sun)

亻 (dānrénpáng, person)

三、组词:
Form words:

休( )　　　　　期( )

起( )　　　　　面( )

再( )　　　　　关( )

现( )　　　　　早( )

四、看拼音写汉字:
Write the Chinese characters represented by the *Pinyin*:

Jīntiān xīngqī jǐ?

Wǒmen shénme shíhou jiànmiàn?

Duìbuqǐ, wǒ jīntiān hěn máng, bù néng gēn nǐ yìqǐ qù dǎ qiú.

五、猜一猜下面的句子是什么意思:
Guess the meanings of the following sentences:

今天晚上我有一个约会。

我现在没有空,你明天上午来,行吗?

休息的时候,他喜欢跟同事一起去喝咖啡。

他约我明天晚上跟他见面,可是没有说在哪儿见面,只说晚上七点三刻来我家接我,让我在家里等他。

多义字 duōyìzì Polysemous characters

If one character is used in different words, it may have approximately the same meaning, as 工 in 工人, 工作, 打工. But sometimes the same Chinese character is used with different meanings in different words, as the 面 of 见面 and 吃面条. In these cases, 面 is called a polysemous character. Another example is the polysemous character 米. It means "rice" in the words 大米 and 米饭, while it means "metre" in 一千三百米 (here 米 is the transliteration of metre).

-儿

Retroflex finals are indicated by the character 儿 in such expressions as 玩儿, 空儿. Except in the case of 这儿, 那儿 and 哪儿, one needs not write retroflex endings, though they appear in the spoken language. For example, instead of 明天我有空儿 we can write 明天我有空.

Dì-qī Kè

第七课

Lesson Seven

汉字

1. 进 7 jìn come/go in, enter 進

进 进 辻 进 讲 讲 进

井 + 辶

进口 进来 进去

请进!

---

2. 放 8 fàng release, put

放 放 放 放 放 放 放 放

方 + 攵

放假 放心 put one's mind at rest, rest assured

放哪儿 put where

3. * 假 11 jià holiday

假 假 假 假 假 假 假 假 假 假

亻 + 段

放假　假日　holiday

---

4. * 旬 6 Ⓑ xún a period of ten days of a month

旬 旬 旬 旬 旬 旬

上旬　中旬　下旬

---

5. 后 6 Ⓑ hòu behind 後

后 后 后 后 后 后

以后　然后　after that, then

---

6. 旅 10 Ⓑ lǚ

旅 旅 旅 旅 旅 旅 旅 旅 旅 旅

方 + 㫃

旅行

---

7. 或 8 huò or

或 或 或 或 或 或 或 或

或者

8. 者　8　Ⓑ　zhě

者 者 者 者 者 者 者 者

　少 ＋ 日

◆ 或者

---

9. 回　6　Ⓑ　huí　be back

回 回 回 回 回 回

◆ 回来　回去

Shows a whirlpool.

---

10. 号　5　hào　number　號

号 号 号 号 号

　口 ＋ 丂

◆ 号码　402号　一月三号

---

11. 前　9　Ⓑ　qián　front

前 前 前 前 前 前 前 前 前

　丷 ＋ 月 ＋ 刂

◆ 以前

---

12. 担　8　Ⓑ　dān　擔

担 担 担 担 担 担 担 担

　扌 ＋ 旦

◆ 担心

13. 心 4 xīn heart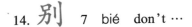

　　心 心 心 心
　　担心　好心　good intentions　小心　careful　中心　centre

14. 别 7 bié don't …

　　别 别 别 别 别 别 别
　　另 ＋ 刂
　　你别担心。

15. 帮 9 bāng 幫

　　帮 帮 帮 帮 帮 帮 帮 帮 帮
　　邦 ＋ 巾
　　帮助

16. 助 7 Ⓑ zhù

　　助 助 助 助 助 助 助
　　且 ＋ 力
　　帮助

17. 找 7 zhǎo look for

　　找 找 找 找 找 找 找
　　扌 ＋ 戈
　　Note: Pay attention to the difference between 找 and 我.
　　找东西　找人
　　你找谁？

18. * 戴　17　dài　wear (hat, watch, gloves, glasses)

戴 戴 戴 戴 戴 戴 戴 戴 戴 戴 戴 戴 戴 戴 戴 戴 戴

戋 ＋ 田 ＋ 共

戴眼镜

---

19. * 副　11　fù

副 副 副 副 副 副 副 副 副 副 副 副

畐 ＋ 刂

一副眼镜

---

20. 眼　11　yǎn　eye

眼 眼 眼 眼 眼 眼 眼 眼 眼 眼 眼

目 ＋ 艮

眼镜　眼睛　yǎnjing　eye

别眼红　don't be envious

---

21. * 镜　16　Ⓑ　jìng　　鏡

镜 镜 镜 镜 镜 镜 镜 镜 镜 镜 镜 镜 镜 镜 镜 镜

钅 ＋ 竟

眼镜

---

22. 每　7　měi　every

每 每 每 每 每 每 每

𠂉 ＋ 母

每天　每年　每个月　每个人

23. * 瘦　14　shòu　thin, lean

瘦 瘦 瘦 瘦 瘦 瘦 瘦 瘦 瘦 瘦 瘦 瘦 瘦 瘦

广　＋　叟

他很瘦。

24. 头　5　tóu　head　頭

头　头　头　头　头

头发

25. 发　5　Ⓑ　fà　hair　髮 ；　fā　send　發

发　发　发　发　发

头发　发电子邮件

26. 长　4　cháng　long　長

长　长　长　长

头发很长

A person with long hair.

27. 穿　9　chuān　wear

穿 穿 穿 穿 穿 穿 穿 穿 穿

宀　＋　牙

穿衣服

28. * 仔 5 Ⓑ zǎi

　　仔　仔　仔　仔　仔

◆　牛仔　cowboy

---

29. 刚 6 gāng only a short while ago, just 剛

　　刚　刚　刚　刚　刚　刚

　　冈　+　刂

◆　他刚回来。　他刚出去。

---

30. 出 5 Ⓑ chū come/go out

　　出　出　出　出　出

◆　出来　出去　出口

---

31. 过 6 guo cross, pass, after 過

　　过　过　过　过　过　过

　　寸　+　辶

◆　请你过一会儿再来。

---

32. 年 6 nián year

　　年　午　午　午　年　年

A man carrying the ripe crops
to his home, meaning "hearvest".

◆　2005年　一年　去年　今年　明年

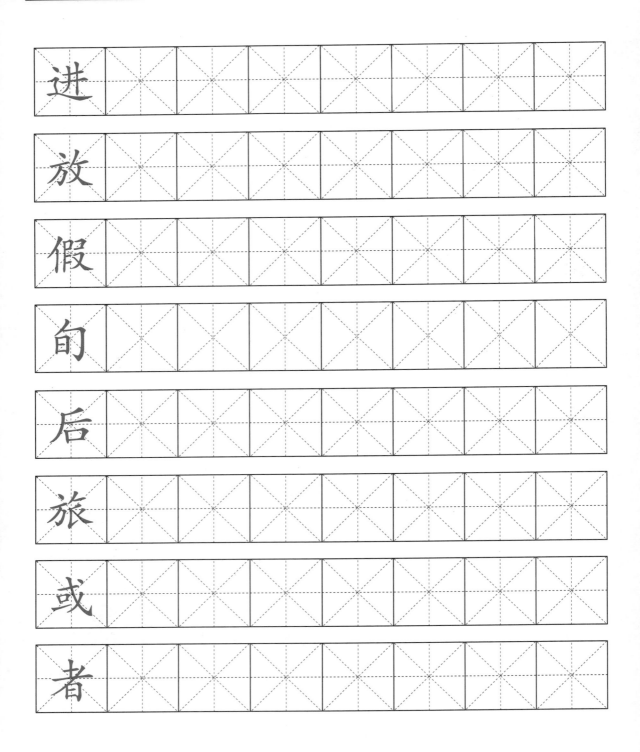

进
放
假
旬
后
旅
或
者

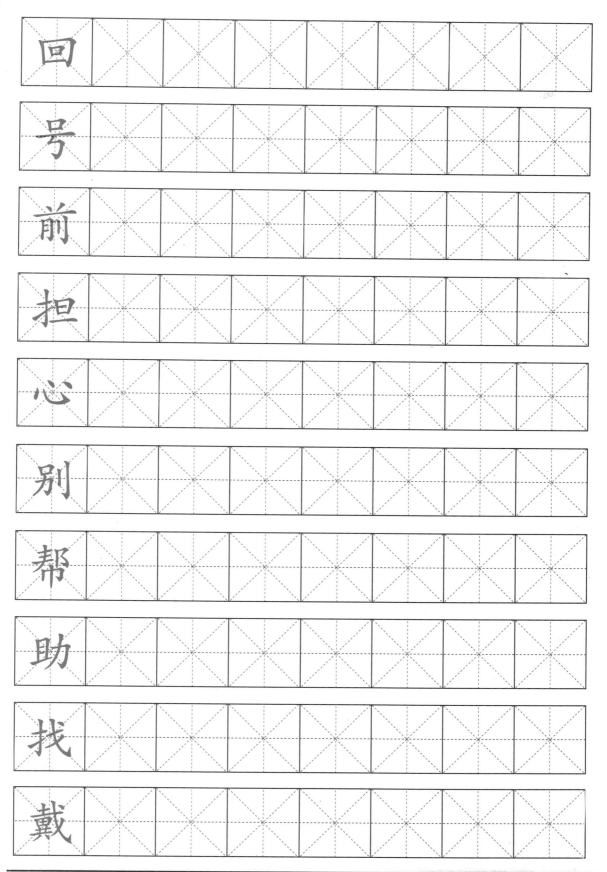

回

号

前

担

心

别

帮

助

找

戴

副

眼

镜

每

瘦

头

发

长

穿

仔

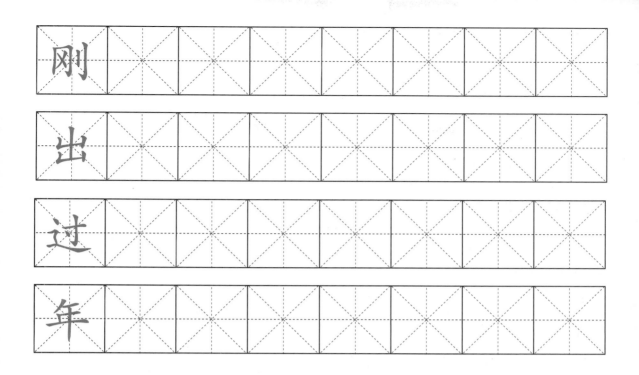

一、比较下列汉字，并注上拼音：

Give the *Pinyin* for these pairs of similar characters：

这（　　　）　　　还（　　　）　　　过（　　　）

头（　　　）　　　买（　　　）　　　卖（　　　）

我（　　　）　　　找（　　　）　　　放（　　　）　　旅（　　　）

刚（　　　）　　　别（　　　）　　　眼（　　　）　　跟（　　　）

者（　　　）　　　都（　　　）　　　长（　　　）　　张（　　　）

二、补上遗漏的笔画：

Supply the missing strokes:

发　　旅　　与　　年　　穿

三、写出含有下列偏旁的汉字：

Write Chinese characters containing the following radicals:

目（mùzìpáng，eye）

扌（tíshǒupáng，hand）

辶（zǒuzhī，walk）

心（xīnzìdǐ，heart）

四、组词：

Form words:

帮（　　　）　　　　头（　　　）

以（　　　）　　　　心（　　　）

或（　　　）　　　　放（　　　）

担（　　　）　　　　旅（　　　）

五、看拼音写汉字：

Write the Chinese characters represented by the *Pinyin*：

Jīntiān jǐ yuè jǐ hào?

Nǐ bié dānxīn, wǒ kěyǐ bāngzhù nǐ.

Tā gāng chūqu, nǐ guò yíhuìr zài lái ba.

六、猜一猜下面的句子是什么意思：

Guess the meanings of the following sentences：

他每天吃很多肉，可是很瘦。

放假以后我打算先去打工，再用打工的钱去旅行。

他六十多岁，不太高，白头发，戴一副眼镜，穿一件红衬衫。

他让我进去，我让他出来。他说："你不进来，我不出去。"我说："你不出来，我不进去。"

Points about Chinese characters

As a result of the long history of Chinese characters, the same Chinese character may be written several different ways which are called variants. For example 回 can be written in several ways: 回 囬 㘞

The standardized written form is 回. In fact, the simple forms of Chinese characters are variants which follow the rules of simplification.

Dì-bā Kè

第八课

Lesson Eight

汉字

1.* 附 7 Ⓑ fù

附 附 附 附 附 附 附

阝 + 付

附近

银行在我家附近。 我家附近有一个银行。

2. 近 7 jìn near

近 近 近 近 近 近 近

辶 + 斤

附近 我家离学校很近。 近视(眼) near-sighted

最近 recently

3. 银　11 Ⓑ yín　silver　銀

　　银 银 银 银 银 银 银 银 银 银 银

　　钅 ＋ 艮

　　银行　银子 silver

4. * 离　10　lí　away from　離

　　离 离 离 离 离 离 离 离 离 离

　　亠 ＋ 凶 ＋ 禸

Shows a bird being taken from a net.

　　这儿离市中心有多远？　现在离放假还有一个月。

5. 远　7 yuǎn　far　遠

　　远 远 远 远 远 远 远

　　元 ＋ 辶

　　我家离学校很远。　多远？　How far?

6. 走　7 zǒu　walk, go

　　走 走 走 走 走 走 走

　　咱们走吧!　Let's go.

Drawing of a man walking and swinging his arms. The upper part 土 (tǔ) derives from the drawing of the walking man. There is a symbol of a footprint under the walking man.

7. 往　8　wǎng　towards

往 往 往 往 往 往 往 往

彳　+　主

往前　　往那边走

8. 边　5　Ⓑ　biān　side　邊

边 边 边 边 边

力　+　辶

里边　外边　左边　前边

旁边　马路边　by the road

请这边走。　This way please.

9. 右　5　Ⓑ　yòu　right

右 右 右 右 右

右边　右面

10.*拐　8　guǎi　turn

拐 拐 拐 拐 拐 拐 拐 拐

扌　+　另

往左拐　往右拐

11. 路　13　lù　road

　　路路路路路路路路路路路路路

　　足　+　各

　　马路　铁路　railway　公路　highway, road　路口　crossing

---

12. 就　12　jiù

　　就就就就就就就就就就就就

　　京　+　尤

　　他就是你要找的人。　前面就是我家。

13. *邮　7　Ⓑ　yóu　郵

　　邮邮邮邮邮邮邮

　　由　+　阝

　　邮件　邮局

14. *局　7　jú　bureau

　　局局局局局局局

　　邮局

15. 旁　10　Ⓑ　páng beside

　　旁旁旁旁旁旁旁旁旁旁

　　亠　+　冖　+　方

　　旁边　汽车在马路旁边等你们。

16. 客 9 Ⓑ kè

客 客 客 客 客 客 客 客 客

宀 + 各

客气　客人 guest　旅客 traveler

17. 气 4 Ⓑ qì gas, air

气 气 气 气

Vapor on the surface of a lake.

客气　天气 weather　空气 kōngqì air

生气 take offense, get angry; vitality　别生我的气。

18. 市 5 shì city

市 市 市 市 市

北京市　市中心 downtown

19. 告 7 Ⓑ gào

告 告 告 告 告 告

生 + 口

告诉

20. 诉 7 Ⓑ sù 訴

诉 诉 诉 诉 诉 诉 诉

讠 + 斤

告诉

21.* 铁 10 tiě iron 鐵

　铁 铁 铁 铁 铁 铁 铁 铁 铁 铁

　钅 ＋ 失

　地铁　铁路 railway

22. 从 4 cóng from 從

　从 从 从 从

　你从哪儿来？　从来不… never

One person following another.

23. 到 8 dào to; until; arrive

　到 到 到 到 到 到 到 到

　至 ＋ 刂

　你到哪儿去？　从这儿到那儿
　从星期一到星期五　你什么时候到学校？

24. 公 4 Ⓑ gōng

　公 公 公 公

　公司　公共 public

25. 共 6 Ⓑ gòng

　共 共 共 共 共 共

Two hands making an offering.

　公共　一共(in all, altogether)多少钱？

26. 汽　7　Ⓑ　qì　vapor, steam

　　汽 汽 汽 汽 汽 汽 泸 汽

　　氵　+　气

　　汽车

27. 车　4　chē　vehicle　車

　　车 车 车 车

　　公共汽车　自行车　　电车　tram, trolley

28. 站　10　zhàn　stand, stop, station

　　站 站 站 站 站 站 站 站 站

　　立　+　占

　　车站　站在前面　站起来　stand up

29. *换　10　huàn　change

　　换 换 换 换 换 换 换 换 换

　　扌　+　奂

　　换钱　换工作　换人　换车

30. 骑　11　qí　ride, sit on the back of　騎

　　骑 马 马 骑 骑 骑 骑 骑 骑

　　马　+　奇

　　骑马　骑自行车　骑车

31. 自　6　Ⓑ　zì　self

自 自 自 自 自 自

自行车　大自然 nature　自己 zìjǐ oneself

32. 左　5　Ⓑ　zuǒ　left

左 左 左 左 左

左面　左边　两个月左右 two months or so

33. 外　5　Ⓑ　wài　outside

外 外 外 外 外

外面　外国　外国人　外语

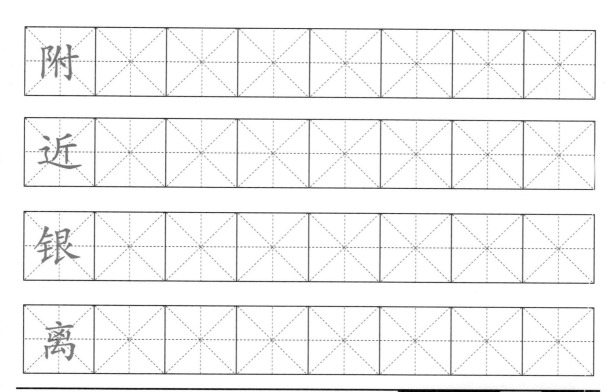

远

走

往

边

右

拐

路

就

邮

局

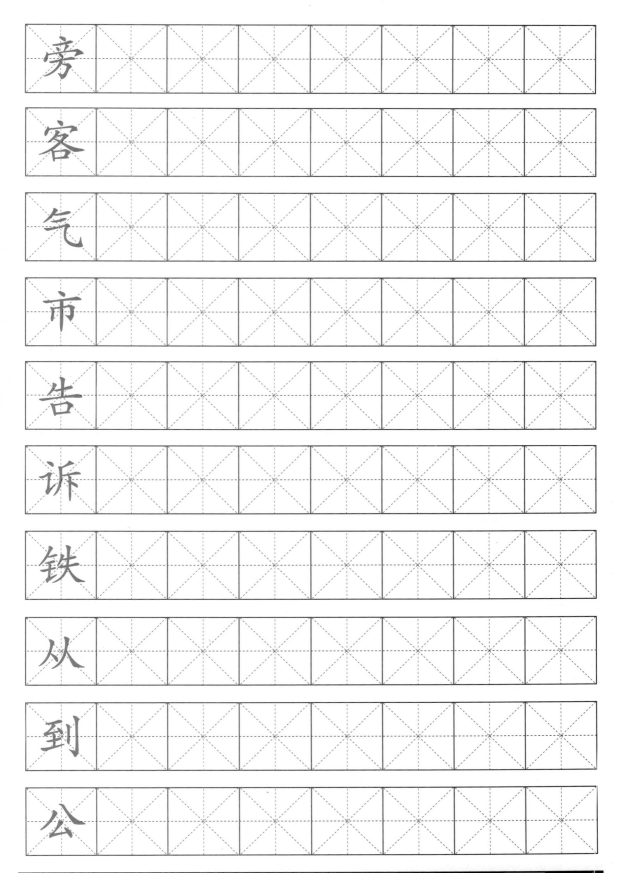

旁

客

气

市

告

诉

铁

从

到

公

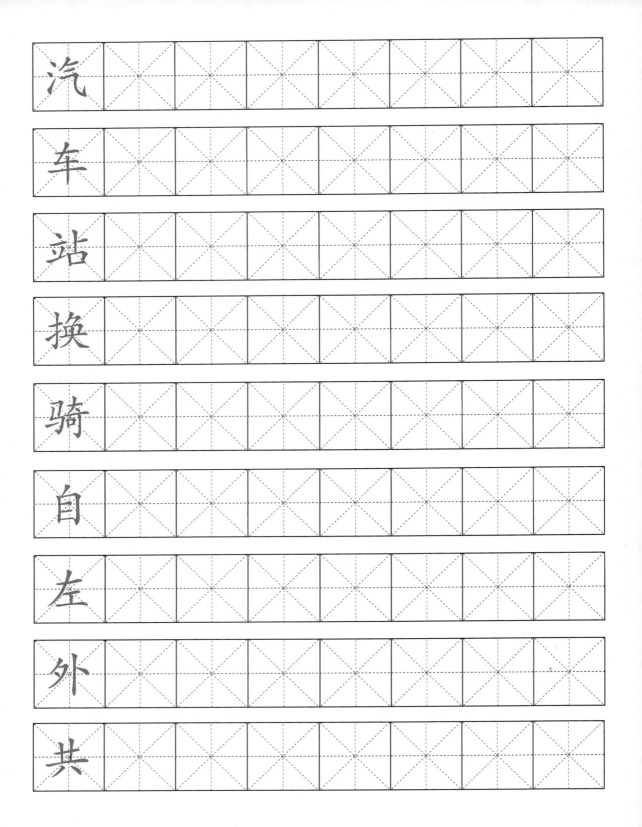

汽

车

站

换

骑

白

左

外

共

一、写出含有下列部件的汉字：

Write Chinese characters containing the following components:

艮　方　马　京　走

二、比较下列汉字，并注上拼音：

Give the *Pinyin* for these pairs of similar characters：

东（　　　）　　　　车（　　　）

么（　　　）　　　　公（　　　）

气（　　　）　　　　汽（　　　）

白（　　　）　　　　自（　　　）　　　　百（　　　　）

左（　　　）　　　　右（　　　）　　　　在（　　　　）

三、补上遗漏的笔画：

Supply the missing strokes:

列　就　诉　亣　庑　沾

四、组词：

Form words:

告（　　　　）　　　　自（　　　　）

气（　　　　）　　　　汽（　　　　）

旁（　　　　）　　　　外（　　　　）

五、看拼音写汉字：

Write the Chinese characters represented by the *Pinyin*:

Wǒmen xuéxiào pángbiān yǒu yí gè yínháng.

Nǐ zuò gōnggòng qìchē qù háishi qí zìxíngchē qù?.

Tā gàosu wǒ, qiánmiàn jiù shì qìchē zhàn.

六、猜一猜下面的句子是什么意思：

Guess the meanings of the following sentences：

银行里的人非常客气，他们从来不生气。

往前走,到第三个路口往左拐，再走五六分钟，就到了。

我家在市中心。我家右面有一个银行，银行旁边有一个邮局,邮局对面有一个商店,商店左面有一个饭店,我常常去那个饭店吃饭。

Points about Chinese characters

多音字　Duōyīnzì　Polyphonous characters

Some Chinese characters can be pronounced in more than one way. For example, 行 sometimes can be read xíng (as in 自行车)；sometimes it can be read háng (as in 银行). This kind of character is called a polyphonous character. Thus,we should first know which word the character is in before we can decide how to pronounce it.

*　　　　　　*　　　　　　*　　　　　　*

车 is a general word for vehicles and is contained in the following words:火车,汽车,摩托车. Similar examples follow:

小学、中学、大学

早饭、中饭/午饭、晚饭

牛肉、羊肉、猪肉、鸡肉……

足球、篮球、排球、冰球、橄榄球、网球……

啤酒、葡萄酒、白酒、黄酒……

In this sense, it is easier to learn Chinese than to learn English. Believe it or not, there are many other easier and more logical aspects in Chinese than in other languages, e.g., the numerals, that you will gradually realize along the way of your Chinese study.

汉字索引　Index of Chinese Characters

A star * on the upper right side of a character indicates that it is optional (i.e., you are required to read it but not to write it). Characters not marked in this way are compulsory (244 in total, all of which you must learn to read and write). The number after a character indicates the lesson in which it first occurs. If a character that was optional in an earlier lesson becomes compulsory in a later lesson, then the first number refers to the lesson in which it becomes compulsory and the number in parentheses refers to the lesson in which it first appeared.

1. 爱 3
2. 八 0
3. 吧 *3
4. 爸 3
5. 白 5
6. 百 3
7. 板 *3
8. 半 6
9. 帮 7
10. 本 4
11. 比 4
12. 笔 *4
13. 边 8
14. 别 7
15. 不 1
16. 菜 *5
17. 茶 *2
18. 长 7
19. 常 4
20. 车 8
21. 衬 *5

22. 吃 5
23. 出 7(2)
24. 穿 7
25. 词 *4
26. 从 8
27. 醋 *5
28. 打 2
29. 大 0
30. 戴 *7
31. 担 7
32. 当 *4
33. 到 8
34. 道 4
35. 的 2
36. 等 5
37. 地 3
38. 典 *4
39. 点 5
40. 电 2
41. 店 5
42. 东 5

43. 都 1
44. 对 4
45. 多 3
46. 儿 2
47. 二 0
48. 发 7(2)
49. 法 *1
50. 饭 5
51. 方 3
52. 放 7
53. 非 4
54. 啡 *6
55. 分 6(3)
56. 服 5
57. 附 *8
58. 副 *7
59. 概 *3
60. 干 4
61. 刚 7
62. 高 2
63. 告 8

64. 个 8
65. 给 4(2)
66. 跟 (6)
67. 工 2
68. 公 8(2/3)
69. 功 *6
70. 共 8
71. 拐 *8
72. 关 6
73. 贵 5 (1)
74. 国 0
75. 过 7
76. 孩 *3
77. 汉 0
78. 好 0
79. 号 7(2)
80. 喝 *2
81. 和 3
82. 河 0
83. 很 2
84. 红 5

85. 后 7	117. 客 8	149. 面 6	181. 人 0
86. 候 6	118. 课 4	150. 名 1	182. 认 *2
87. 话 2	119. 空 6	151. 明 0	183. 日 0
88. 欢 *2	120. 口 0	152. 木 0	184. 肉 5
89. 还 1	121. 裤 *5/7	153. 哪 2(1)	185. 三 0
90. 换 *8	122. 块 *5	154. 那 2	186. 山 4
91. 回 7	123. 辣 *5	155. 男 2	187. 衫 *5
92. 会 5	124. 来 5	156. 呢 1	188. 商 *5
93. 或 7	125. 老 1	157. 能 4	189. 上 0
94. 几 3	126. 离 *8	158. 你 1	190. 烧 5
95. 家 3	127. 里 6(2)	159. 年 7	191. 少 3
96. 假 *7	128. 两 3	160. 您 1	192. 生 3
97. 见 6	129. 亮 2	161. 牛 5	193. 师 1
98. 件 *2/5	130. 了 5	162. 女 0	194. 十 0
99. 饺 *5	131. 林 0	163. 旁 8	195. 什 1
100. 叫 1	132. 六 0	164. 朋 2	196. 时 6
101. 较 4	133. 龙 *4	165. 便 5	197. 识 *2
102. 教 *4	134. 路 8	166. 漂 2	198. 市 8
103. 接 *6	135. 旅 7	167. 七 0	199. 事 6
104. 她 1	136. 妈 0	168. 期 6	200. 视 *6
105. 姐 5	137. 马 0	169. 骑 8	201. 试 *5
106. 今 6	138. 码 *2	170. 起 6	202. 室 *4
107. 近 8	139. 吗 1	171. 气 8	203. 是 1
108. 进 7(2)	140. 买 5	172. 汽 8	204. 瘦 *7
109. 镜 *7	141. 卖 5	173. 千 3	205. 书 4
110. 九 0	142. 忙 6	174. 前 7	206. 谁 4
111. 就 8	143. 么 1	175. 钱 5	207. 水 0
112. 局 *8	144. 没 3	176. 请 2	208. 说 1
113. 咖 *6	145. 每 7	177. 球 6	209. 司 *2/3
114. 看 4	146. 门 0	178. 去 3	210. 思 *4
115. 可 2	147. 们 1	179. 然 *4/8	211. 四 0
116. 刻 *6	148. 米 5	180. 让 3	212. 诉 8

213. 酸 *5	238. 五 0	263. 要 4	288. 早 6
214. 算 *6	239. 午 6	264. 也 1	289. 怎 2
215. 岁 3	240. 西 5	265. 一 0	290. 站 8
216. 他 1	241. 息 6	266. 衣 5	291. 张 4
217. 太 3	242. 习 0	267. 宜 5	292. 找 7
218. 汤 *5	243. 喜 *2	268. 以 2	293. 者 7
219. 糖 *5	244. 系 6(2)	269. 意 * 4	294. 这 2
220. 天 0	245. 下 0	270. 因 3	295. 真 4
221. 田 0	246. 先 5	271. 银 8	296. 支 *4
222. 条 *5	247. 现 6	272. 英 4(1)	297. 知 4
223. 铁 *8	248. 想 3	273. 走 8	298. 只 1
224. 同 1	249. 小 0	274. 用 4	299. 中 0
225. 头 7	250. 校 3	275. 邮 *2/8	300. 钟 *6
226. 图 4	251. 写 0	276. 友 2	301. 助 7
227. 外 8	252. 谢 *2	277. 有 3	302. 子 0
228. 玩 4	253. 心 7	278. 右 8	303. 字 0
229. 晚 6	254. 兴 2	279. 鱼 *5	304. 自 8
230. 万 3	255. 星 6	280. 语 0	305. 走 8
231. 王 0	256. 行 4	281. 远 8	306. 最 5
232. 往 8	257. 姓 1	282. 院 *2	307. 左 8
233. 为 3	258. 休 6	283. 约 * 6	308. 作 2
234. 位 *6	259. 学 0	284. 月 0	309. 坐 2
235. 文 0	260. 旬 *7	285. 仔 *7	310. 做 6
236. 问 4	261. 眼 7	286. 再 6	
237. 我 1	262. 样 2	287. 在 2	

漢字索引　**Index of Chinese Characters**

A star * on the upper right side of a character indicates that it is optional (i.e., you are required to read it but not to write it).Characters not marked in this way are compulsory （244 in total， all of which you must learn to read and write）． The number after a character indicates the lesson in which it first occurs． If a character that was optional in an earlier lesson becomes compulsory in a later lesson， then the first number refers to the lesson in which it becomes compulsory and the number in parentheses refers to the lesson in which it first appeared．

1. 愛 3
2. 八 0
3. 吧 *3
4. 爸 3
5. 白 5
6. 百 3
7. 板 *3
8. 半 6
9. 幫 7
10. 本 4
11. 比 4
12. 筆 *4
13. 邊 8
14. 別 7
15. 不 1
16. 菜 *5
17. 茶 *2
18. 長 7
19. 常 4
20. 車 8
21. 襯 *5

22. 吃 5
23. 出 7(2)
24. 穿 7
25. 詞 *4
26. 從 8
27. 醋 *5
28. 打 2
29. 大 0
30. 戴 *7
31. 擔 7
32. 當 *4
33. 到 8
34. 道 4
35. 的 2
36. 等 5
37. 地 3
38. 典 *4
39. 點 5
40. 電 2
41. 店 5
42. 東 5

43. 都 1
44. 對 4
45. 多 3
46. 兒 2
47. 二 0
48. 發 7(2)
49. 法 *1
50. 飯 5
51. 方 3
52. 放 7
53. 非 4
54. 啡 *6
55. 分 6(3)
56. 服 5
57. 附 *8
58. 副 *7
59. 概 *3
60. 干 4
61. 剛 7
62. 高 2
63. 告 8

64. 個 8
65. 給 4(2)
66. 跟(6)
67. 工 2
68. 公 8(2/3)
69. 功 *6
70. 共 8
71. 拐 *8
72. 關 6
73. 貴 5 (1)
74. 國 0
75. 過 7
76. 孩 *3
77. 漢 0
78. 好 0
79. 號 7(2)
80. 喝 *2
81. 和 3
82. 河 0
83. 很 2
84. 紅 5

85. 後 7	117. 客 8	149. 面 6	181. 人 0
86. 候 6	118. 課 4	150. 名 1	182. 認 *2
87. 話 2	119. 空 6	151. 明 0	183. 日 0
88. 歡 *2	120. 口 0	152. 木 0	184. 肉 5
89. 還 1	121. 褲 *5/7	153. 哪 2(1)	185. 三 0
90. 換 *8	122. 塊 *5	154. 那 2	186. 山 4
91. 回 7	123. 辣 *5	155. 男 2	187. 衫 *5
92. 會 5	124. 來 5	156. 呢 1	188. 商 *5
93. 或 7	125. 老 1	157. 能 4	189. 上 0
94. 幾 3	126. 離 *8	158. 你 1	190. 燒 5
95. 家 3	127. 里 6(2)	159. 年 7	191. 少 3
96. 假 *7	128. 兩 3	160. 您 1	192. 生 3
97. 見 6	129. 亮 2	161. 牛 5	193. 師 1
98. 件 *2/5	130. 了 5	162. 女 0	194. 十 0
99. 餃 *5	131. 林 0	163. 旁 8	195. 什 1
100. 叫 1	132. 六 0	164. 朋 2	196. 時 6
101. 較 4	133. 龍 *4	165. 便 5	197. 識 *2
102. 教 *4	134. 路 8	166. 漂 2	198. 市 8
103. 接 *6	135. 旅 7	167. 七 0	199. 事 6
104. 她 1	136. 媽 0	168. 期 6	200. 視 *6
105. 姐 5	137. 馬 0	169. 騎 8	201. 試 *5
106. 今 6	138. 碼 *2	170. 起 6	202. 室 *4
107. 近 8	139. 嗎 1	171. 氣 8	203. 是 1
108. 進 7(2)	140. 買 5	172. 汽 8	204. 瘦 *7
109. 鏡 *7	141. 賣 5	173. 千 3	205. 書 4
110. 九 0	142. 忙 6	174. 前 7	206. 誰 4
111. 就 8	143. 么 1	175. 錢 5	207. 水 0
112. 局 *8	144. 沒 3	176. 請 2	208. 說 1
113. 咖 *6	145. 每 7	177. 球 6	209. 司 *2/3
114. 看 4	146. 門 0	178. 去 3	210. 思 *4
115. 可 2	147. 們 1	179. 然 *4/8	211. 四 0
116. 刻 *6	148. 米 5	180. 讓 3	212. 訴 8

213. 酸 *5	238. 五 0	263. 要 4	288. 早 6
214. 算 *6	239. 午 6	264. 也 1	289. 怎 2
215. 歲 3	240. 西 5	265. 一 0	290. 站 8
216. 他 1	241. 息 6	266. 衣 5	291. 張 4
217. 太 3	242. 習 0	267. 宜 5	292. 找 7
218. 湯 *5	243. 喜 *2	268. 以 2	293. 者 7
219. 糖 *5	244. 系 6（2）	269. 意 * 4	294. 這 2
220. 天 0	245. 下 0	270. 因 3	295. 眞 4
221. 田 0	246. 先 5	271. 銀 8	296. 支 *4
222. 條 *5	247. 現 6	272. 英 4（1）	297. 知 4
223. 鐵 *8	248. 想 3	273. 走 8	298. 祇 1
224. 同 1	249. 小 0	274. 用 4	299. 中 0
225. 頭 7	250. 校 3	275. 郵 *2/8	300. 鐘 *6
226. 圖 4	251. 寫 0	276. 友 2	301. 助 7
227. 外 8	252. 謝 *2	277. 有 3	302. 子 0
228. 玩 4	253. 心 7	278. 右 8	303. 字 0
229. 晚 6	254. 興 2	279. 魚 *5	304. 自 8
230. 萬 3	255. 星 6	280. 語 0	305. 走 8
231. 王 0	256. 行 4	281. 遠 8	306. 最 5
232. 往 8	257. 姓 1	282. 院 *2	307. 左 8
233. 爲 3	258. 休 6	283. 約 * 6	308. 作 2
234. 位 *6	259. 學 0	284. 月 0	309. 坐 2
235. 文 0	260. 旬 *7	285. 仔 *7	310. 做 6
236. 問 4	261. 眼 7	286. 再 6	
237. 我 1	262. 樣 2	287. 在 2	

《当代中文》系列教材（全14册）
Contemporary Chinese Series（14 volumes）

《当代中文》课本（共4册）
Contemporary Chinese — Textbook (4 volumes)

- 课本共4册，每册12课，每册可供一学期或一学年学完。
- 课文配有图画、照片等，简繁对照，附拼音文本和英语翻译。
- Totaled 4 volumes of textbooks. Each book consists of 12 lessons for one term or one year.
- Accompanied with pictures and photos and explained in both simple and traditional Chinese characters, pinyin and English translation, the texts are interesting and practical.

《当代中文》汉字本（共2册）
Contemporary Chinese — Character Book (2 volumes)

- 汉字本共2册，1册汉字310个，2册汉字371个。
- 全书提供汉字的有关知识，多种多样的练习材料，简体字、繁体字的汉字索引等内容。
- 2 accompanied Character Books. Book I. includes 310 most-commonly used Chinese characters and Book II. includes 371 characters.
- The books provide relevant language points of Chinese characters and various forms of exercises. Index of simple Chinese characters and traditional ones are also included.

《当代中文》练习册（共4册）
Contemporary Chinese — Exercise Book (4 volumes)

- 练习材料包括听、说、读、写、译各个方面，难易结合，兼顾学习者的不同需求和水平。
- The 4 accompanied exercise books cover the training of listening and speaking, writing, and translation. It can meets the requirements of students of different language levels.

《当代中文》教师手册（共4册）
Contemporary Chinese — Teachers' Book (4 volumes)

- 教师手册共4册，详细说明编者的设计意图，教材的整体构架、使用建议及有关参考资料，以及听力材料书面文本、练习答案、试卷等等。
- There are 4 volumes of teachers' books giving a detailed explanation to the outline of the textbooks and the advice on how to use the textbooks. The scripts of the listening materials and keys to exercises are also provided.

配套CD（共4套）
Accompanied CD (4 sets)

配套CD-ROM（共4套）
Accompanied CD-ROM (4 sets)

配套DVD（共4套）
Accompanied DVD (4 sets)

责任编辑：贾寅淮
封面设计：王　博
插　图：笑　龙
印刷监制：佟汉冬

《当代中文》

汉字本

1

主编　吴中伟

*

© 华语教学出版社
华语教学出版社出版
（中国北京百万庄大街 24 号　邮政编码100037）
电话：010-68320585　68997826
传真：010-68997826　68326333
网址：www.sinolingua.com.cn
电子信箱：hyjx@sinolingua.com.cn
北京外文印刷厂印刷
2003年（16开）第 1 版
2011 年第 7 次印刷
（汉英）
ISBN 978-7-80052-881-1
9-CE-3520PA
定价：48.50 元